The Smart Mom's Guide to Staying Home

The Smart Mom's Guide to Staying Home

65 Simple Ways to Thrive, Not Deprive, on One Income

By

CHRISTINE K. WALKER

National Library of Canada Cataloguing in Publication Walker, Christine, 1967- The smart mom's guide to staying home : 65 simple ways to thrive, not deprive, on one income / Christine Walker.
ISBN 1-4120-0760-7 I.
Title. TX326.W34 2003   332.024   C2003-903843-2

TRAFFORD

This book was published on-demand in cooperation with Trafford Publishing. On-demand publishing is a unique process and service of making a book available for retail sale to the public taking advantage of on-demand manufacturing and Internet marketing. On-demand publishing includes promotions, retail sales, manufacturing, order fulfillment, accounting and collecting royalties on behalf of the author

Suite 6E, 2333 Government St., Victoria, B.C. V8T 4P4, CANADA
Phone   250-383-6864   Toll-free 1-888-232-4444 (Canada & US)
Fax   250-383-6804   E-mail   sales@trafford.com
Web site www.trafford.com

TRAFFORD PUBLISHING IS A DIVISION OF TRAFFORD HOLDINGS LTD.
Trafford Catalogue #03-1128
www.trafford.com/robots/03-1128.html
10   9   8   7   6   5   4   3   2

Contents

Preface

As the saying goes, "Money makes the world go around." If that's the case, each of us has to have enough money to get us where we want to go. If we lack the funds we need, we either have to make more money, or spend less money. Spending less, however, does *not* have to mean going without. *The Smart Mom's Guide to Staying Home* is meant to provide resources for families to thrive on one income.

Being a stay-at-home mom takes some major planning and doesn't come about overnight. The very fact that you picked up this book shows that you have already given some thought to making things work financially. Your heart is probably committed to making the jump, but maybe you're still not sure how smoothly things will go without your income. You have probably taken the time to write down what your net income is after all your child care, transportation and other work-related expenses have been taken out. What you actually net is most likely a negligible amount when you consider what you are giving up to bring that home. So, now that you've made the decision that's right for you, come along for a ride that will show you how you can be what you want, go where you want and do it all with money to spare!

The purpose of this book is to help parents who want to stay home and make their families their first priority. A recent survey in *Parents* magazine found that 87% of U.S. mothers with children 12 and under, who work outside the home, would choose to stay home if they could afford to. This book is written for each woman who feels that her family is her passion and that the greatest gift she can give her children is her time and energy. *The Smart Mom's Guide to Staying Home* also illustrates just how simple it is to stay home with your children, downsize to one income and not feel that you are depriving yourself of anything you value.

After 15 years in the workforce, I traded in my laptop for a double-stroller to stay home with our two young boys, Schuyler, now 3 years old, and Connor, now 1 year old. Many high-profile moms, including former presidential advisor Mary Matalin, have done the same. Mary recently admitted that "the stress of juggling marriage, motherhood and one of the world's most demanding jobs regularly reduced me — and my loved ones — to tears." Mary found herself constantly thinking about her two girls, Matty, 7, and Emma, 4, while working long hours and traveling for days at a time. Instead of putting herself and her family through more strife, Mary left the White House after serving two years as Vice President Dick Cheney's top political advisor. While Mary and her husband, James Carville, didn't have to weigh the financial impact of Mary leaving her full-time job as much as other families do, Mary nonetheless made the decision that was best for her — spending less time away from home and more time with her kids. Mary now works on a few projects each month, rather than putting in 70 hour workweeks. Mary admits that her girls "just like me to be here," referring to her newfound ability to drive the girls to school, go to the movies and just hang out at home.

Many moms who work outside the home can relate to Mary's story. We have all experienced the pain of leaving the house when we would rather stay, or being out of town and missing a milestone or event. Mary's story also provides a good lesson: No job is so important that it can't be done by someone else. *The New York Times Magazine* recently had a cover story on the trend among many well-educated, professional women who are opting out of the workforce to spend more time with their young children. The subtitle of the article was "Abandoning the Climb and Heading Home." The moms in this story speak passionately about their desire to be the ones who shape their children and not delegate the raising of their children to daycare or nannies. Many women spoke of how scaling back work schedules and even delaying corporate advancement was not seen as a sacrifice; they felt pulled toward motherhood and away from jobs with which they grew increasingly dissatisfied. Most women stated that they planned to return to the workforce once their children were older, but wanted to take advantage of those precious early years many women waited decades to experience. Even *The Times* (London) has written about business women who opted out of their high-powered jobs in favor of starting their own businesses in order to spend more time with their small children. If you believe, as these, I and countless other women do, that while there are many other people who can perform your job, only you can be your child's mom, this is the book for you.

In the book *The Two-Income Trap*, authors Elizabeth Warren and Amelia Warren Tyagi challenge the premise that 2 incomes make for a prosperous household. They write, "The average two-income family earns far more than did the single breadwinner family of a generation ago. And yet, once they have paid the mortgage, the car payments, the taxes, the health insurance and the day-care bills, today's dual-income families have *less* discretionary income — and less money to put away for a rainy day. The authors go on to say that a dual-income family becomes accustomed to higher income and lives accordingly. Maintaining this standard of living can be the most challenging aspect of scaling back to one income and the very essence of what this book is about.

In *The Smart Mom's Guide to Staying Home*, you will learn:

* How eating and spending habits are identical.

* How to increase (or start!) your charitable giving.

* How you can wear designer labels and pay just about nothing for them.

* How to save money on everyday purchases, including photo development, toys and magazines.

Most of what I've written is based on a philosophy and lifestyle deeply rooted in frugality. Having this as a starting point was extremely helpful in making the jump from corporate manager to full-time Child Development Specialist (my answer to the "So what do you do?" question. It sounds like a 'real' job and seems to garner a little more respect with adults.) Nonetheless, the real-life, real-world, suggestions I offer are exactly what can allow your family to thrive economically, while maintaining your sanity, every day.

Many authors on family finance espouse depriving yourself, everything from canceling your cable to skipping take-out meals. I have taken a stand against this approach and say, "Don't go without, get it for less!" The last thing that a stay-at-home mom wants to hear is that she has to go without something she wants, or needs. No one has a greater need for support than the stay-at-home mom and, ironically, she's usually the last person to get it. Whether it is a night out, a new haircut or simply having some time alone to enjoy a magazine and a cup of hot tea, these seemingly small things all add up to your quality of life.

In *no* way should this book be interpreted as advocating that ALL women should stay home with their children. Nothing could be further from the truth. Women have worked for years to earn the right to choose what path they would take, either home or work, or some combination of both. Some women have no desire to stay home and find greater fulfillment by focusing on their chosen professions. Rather, I wrote this book to let the overwhelming majority of women who work outside the home who *would prefer to stay home*, that there are some very simple, easy-to-follow ways to do it, all without sacrificing their standard of living.

C.K.W., Evanston, Illinois
Spring 2004

Acknowledgments

This book would not be possible without the support of so many people. First, I dedicate this book to my mom, the original Smart Mom. Her savvy, wisdom and commitment to excellence made me what I am today. I can only hope that I am half the great mom to my boys that she was, and continues to be, to me. To my dear husband, Dave, I thank God for bringing us together on that beautiful September day in 1997. You are the absolute love of my life and I am so grateful that you picked me. To my circle of friends (and you know who you are!), you sustain me. Your love, support and encouragement (and just plain putting up with me) puts me always in your debt. To my sons Schuyler and Connor, I love you more than words can express. I hope you see and feel the love that I have for you and know that everything I do, I do for you. To Trafford Publishing, for making this book a reality. To Bob Bradner of Conversation Press, whose family friendship and professional support set the course for actually getting this book written. To Bonnie Needham, my proofreader. Thank you for making my words not only correct, but better. And to Todd Sanders, for your creativity and vision for making all the graphic elements of this book come together perfectly.

Most importantly, here's to ALL the stay-at-home moms. I honor you, salute you and admire you for the choices you make every day. Only other moms (and dads) in your shoes can truly understand what you give to your job, 24/7. Where else can you get lifetime job security in a position that pays no money, offers no health insurance or 401K, denies you state-mandated breaks and lunchtime, and doesn't cap the amount of hours you can work? Instead of cash, you'll be paid in kisses and sharing of moments that are beyond that of any paycheck. (It's kind of like the country doctor getting paid with chickens and homemade jams.) All that said, the decision to stay at home with your children is perhaps the one decision that you will never regret. You have the most important job on the planet and don't ever let anyone tell you otherwise, or make you feel as though you don't have a "real" job. You'll get so much more out of parenting, your children will benefit tremendously from your full-time presence and the world will be a better place, filled with adults who, as children, had a parent who made raising them their full-time job. Thank you for all you do every day.

Introduction

Since childhood, I have seen maximum-strength frugality first-hand. My great-grandparents were of Scottish descent. Scots, as you may know, are notoriously careful (read: tight) with their money. This trait was not lost on my grandparents, and was perhaps perfected by my mother (one of the quotes in her high-school yearbook was, "I can get it for you wholesale.") I have 2 distinct childhood memories which have not only proven to be a model for my own spending habits, but perhaps best illustrate our family's history of raising frugality to an art form.

As a child, my mom would take me grocery shopping at this great mom and pop store, just a few doors down from our house. She made a point to go only on Saturdays, after 6 pm, when all produce was marked to half price. The store was closed on Sundays and needed to clear whatever perishable inventory it had, hence the slashed prices. Mom always said that it didn't make any sense to pay for a bag of carrots that, hours later, would cost half the price. So, our tradition of grocery shopping dates on Saturday nights began, and continued, for the better part of 3 years.

As for clothes shopping, I got new clothes only twice a year, at the January and August clearance sales. Mom always maintained her high standards of frequenting all the very best department stores (think Bonwit Teller and I. Magnin), while refusing to pay full retail price. We would head straight to the stores following the holidays and hit the clearance sales for winter clothing. I particularly remember a darling forest green winter coat that we bought, which days earlier was nearly twice the price we paid. We would repeat the pilgrimage in late summer and have equal, if not greater, success. Mom would look ahead and try to predict with some accuracy what size I might be in one year, or even two, and gobble up whatever deals she could find. Mom subsequently did the same for her clothing purchases and always looked great. Mom said that she and I looked like a million bucks without spending it. Thus was born a streak of bargain-hunting and sale-only shopping that continues to this day.

Frugality has long been the lifestyle of people from all walks of life, from politicians and celebrities to CEOs. Katie Couric is an unabashed frugal mom, refusing to pay exorbitant prices for just about anything. Katie admits to packing peanut butter and jelly sandwiches for her girls when they travel, as well as checking out most clearance sales for a good deal. On a salary which can best be described as enviable, Katie still spends her money carefully. Legendary songwriter Diane Warren admits that she "still shops at Loehmann's," despite an annual income of more than $20 million. Model Emme admits that she was once "the Queen of the Salvation Army," seeking out great furnishings to outfit her home. And Judith Nathan, wife of Rudy Giuliani, loves a good bargain. Hosting some of the world's most notable guests in their Manhattan home, Nathan boasts that "You can get the best candles and housewares at T.J. Maxx."

President John Adams wrote to his wife, Abigail, "let frugality and industry be our virtues," to which Abigail replied, "I endeavor to live in the most frugal manner possible."

The late former Congressman Bob Stump (R-AZ) shunned the generous office allowance he received to provide for staff and supplies. Instead, he had a bare-bones staff, no press secretary, and often answered his own phone and opened his own mail, all of which are all but unheard of for members of Congress. Not only did this keep Congressman Stump in touch with his constituency, as well as the daily demands of his position, but he also saved the taxpayers more than $500,000 over his 26-year career on Capitol Hill. When he died, his obituary began, "Frugal Former Lawmaker . . ."

The culture of frugality at Amazon.com can be attributed largely to founder and CEO Jeff Bezos, whose net worth exceeds $ 1 billion. Offices at Amazon.com's Seattle corporate headquarters are filled with "door desks," recycled doors lying across stacked milk crates, which also serve as filing cabinets. Billionaire investor Warren Buffet, the second-wealthiest man in the world (with a net worth of more than $36 billion), is also incredibly frugal. As CEO of Berkshire Hathaway in Omaha, Nebraska, Buffet still lives in the house he bought more than 40 years ago for $31,500. Buffet also prefers a burger and Coke at his desk over an expensive power lunch. And not to be outdone, Bill Gates, the world's wealthiest man (with a net worth ringing in at $77 billion), also, has a massive frugal streak. (Legend has it that Warren Buffet and Bill Gates' standard golf bet is $1.) Microsoft provides its managers with frugal budgets for projects and opts for canned cocktail wieners instead of shrimp for parties. Even up until 1998, Bill Gates and Microsoft #2 Steve Ballmer flew coach on business trips. As savvy CEOs understand, the less money spent on non-essentials, the more money you'll have to reinvest in research and development, as well as shareholder profit. The message in these companies is simple: Be frugal and pass the savings on to your customers and shareholders.

The lesson here is that frugality isn't just for those on low incomes or trying to make ends meet. Some of the world's wealthiest people are among the most frugal (maybe that's why they are so rich?) In any event, make frugality your friend and you'll be amazed at how easy it is and how quickly it will become a way of life.

Frugality has allowed our family to live on one income. Dave and I both agree that it is wise to live beneath your means and that there is a huge difference between *spending* money and *having* money. After Dave and I were married in October of 1998, we lived in northwest suburban Chicago. While our location was fine for me, it was an incredibly long commute into the city for Dave, so we agreed that it was time to move closer to his job downtown. When we were house-hunting back in early 2000, just before Schuyler was born, we agreed that we would buy a home that we could afford on only one income. We by-passed large, high-priced single-family homes in favor of a three-bedroom, two-bath condo with all of the amenities we needed. Although we qualified for a larger mortgage, I wasn't sure how I would feel going back to work once the baby came. And with Dave working in the unstable and unpredictable financial markets, we wanted to make sure we could make the mortgage payments if ever one of us wasn't working. This turned out to be a very smart move, as both Dave and I had changes in our job situations.

In addition to doing more for your family, you can be more charitable to less fortunate families. You might think that on less income, all charitable donations would fall by the wayside.

Nothing could be further from the truth! Through careful spending of time and money, I am able to donate to several not-for-profit organizations, civic clubs and faith-based charities. This giving is such a source of joy for me. Knowing that I play a role in enabling a senior citizen to eat a hot meal, keeping a family warm in the winter or even making a Halloween party possible for underprivileged kids is priceless. It is important to me that I continue this as often as I can and gradually increase my level of support. Throughout the book, I'll cover details about how I do it and how you can do the same.

Perhaps the greatest benefit to a frugal mindset is simply being able to sleep at night knowing that you have money in the bank. In the pages to follow, you will see that frugality is a state of mind, not a quick fix, and that savvy spending is about getting it for less, not going without. Making the most out of everything you have will allow you to have the standard of living that your second income provided. I hope you find that the advice and examples in this book help you keep more of what you have and plan for the dreams you've made. If I can do it, YOU can, too!

Living a lifestyle of balanced spending is nearly identical to a lifestyle of balanced eating. Just about everyone has dieted at some point or another. We lose a few pounds, gain a few back and repeat the cycle until we finally get a grip on the key to long-term weight management. It's not about giving up the foods you love and denying yourself any eating pleasures. Bob Greene, Oprah Winfrey's personal trainer, was once asked what foods at McDonald's people should avoid. Bob responded that "one of the worst things you can do is deprive yourself on a routine basis." Bob's approach is right on target, although no one would confuse his comments to mean it's OK to inhale 2 Big Macs every day. It's about balance. What happens when you feel denied? You go overboard. It's been a week of living on lettuce soup, sliced beets and pineapple juice and you've about had it! What are you going to do? Probably head for the nearest box of Ho-Hos and extra-large deep-dish pizza and wolf them down in one sitting. And where are you then? No closer to your weight goal, and more importantly, no better at balancing food needs and wants. Spending money and eating are indeed very much alike. At the core, it's simply about finding the balance between what you want, what you need and what you already have.

Another way to think about your relationship with money and relationship with food is to think about reading a great recipe and trying to figure out how to make it less fattening. At each meal, you have a choice of going full-fat, or low-fat. You *have* to eat, so going *without* food is not an option. What you have to do is make the better choice. As you would consider your food options, you should consider your spending options: a choice at every meal — a choice at every cash register.

Citibank has undertaken an advertising effort of late that stresses not only using credit wisely, but raising awareness of making sound purchasing choices. Mortgage lender Fannie Mae has, too. A commercial has a woman passing a store and whips out her credit card as she is eyeing a pair of new shoes. She then glances over to a real estate office and sees the new homes listed. She slowly walks away from the shoe store as she puts her credit card back in her wallet. This is a great illustration of how putting needs ahead of wants can have incredibly rewarding results. Owning a home was more important to this woman than yet another pair of dress shoes.

There are many easy ways to trim the fat from your waistline as well as your wallet, all without feeling deprived. So, think of this book as "Cooking Light" for your family's finances!

As you'll see, the message of *The Smart Mom's Guide to Staying Home* is unlike any other book you'll find on the topic of family finance. Too many authors insist on "gratification deprivation," going without in order to save money. While watching what you spend is responsible, too much going without makes most of us a little grumpy, especially us moms who already feel that we are underappreciated! The last thing that I want to hear on a particularly trying day is that I can't have something I know would improve my state of mind. Americans don't embrace deprivation anyway. So, I say, "Don't go without, get it for less." There are also some easy routes to pulling in some extra cash as well. And I've offered you 65 simple ways that I do it every day and you can too!

CHAPTER 1

Getting Started

"A journey of 1,000 miles begins
with a single step."

—CONFUCIUS

Frugal vs. Cheap: What's the Difference?

Before we dive into the 65 ways your family can thrive on one income, we first have to take a look at some of the approaches to spending and define our terms. Many people use terms like "frugal" and "cheap" interchangeably, while these two terms are actually worlds apart. Living on one income is based on frugality, not being cheap. As I see it, the key differences between cheap and frugal are:

* Cheap is when you buy the least expensive item offered, regardless of the quality, even when you can afford to pay more. Frugal is when you have means, but are smart enough to shop around for the best price. Frugal people know the retail prices of just about everything and know where, when and how to get the best price.

* Cheap looks cheap; frugal looks full price.

* Cheap is settling for what costs the least; frugal is paying a ridiculously low price for the same item for which someone paid four times as much.

* Cheap is not caring about the longevity of the item you buy;

frugal is knowing that most purchases should be thought of as long-term investments.

* Cheap is frivolous; frugal is practical.

* Cheap is not spending any money even when the need exists; frugal gets the best price possible and buys in quantity to sustain the savings.

* Cheap is a mindset that prevents you from appreciating some of life's finest things, places and people. Frugal sees the opportunities to enjoy, despite the price, knowing their value.

* Cheap thinks of price; frugal thinks of value.

* Cheap deprives; frugal thrives!

Smart Moms understand that you have opportunities to purchase without guilt, pass up when it's best and indulge when necessary, every day.

Wants vs. Needs:
The Second Piece of the Puzzle

Another aspect of frugality is knowing the difference between wants and needs. Purchasing needs should always come ahead of wants. Needs are as short-term as a gallon of milk, or as long-term as a car. Needs add value; wants can diminish value. Needs are clearly defined; wants lack focus. Purchasing needs puts your financial future ahead of the present; purchasing wants often jeopardizes those plans. You plan for needs; wants often surprise you. Wants also creep up on you when you feel deprived and vulnerable. Remember, spending is like eating — when the needs (nutrition) are met, many of the wants (junk food) go away.

Get the picture? The key to really understanding frugality is that it is a mindset, a lifestyle, a commitment. Sounds kind of like managing your weight, doesn't it? That's not by accident. As I mentioned in the Introduction, there are many similarities between spending and eating. As Weight Watchers states, "A healthy body results from a healthy lifestyle."

Essentially, prioritizing wants is the ability to defer gratification. Impulse buying is a good example of wants vs. needs. Say you're doing a bit of window shopping and you see something that catches your eye. Rather than heading into the store and grabbing it, a better thing to do is to walk away. Go home. Think about it for a few days. If you still want the item, and are sure you are getting the best possible price, by all means, head back to the store and buy it. If possible, pay cash or use your debit card.

When someone commits to spending less money, they might tighten their belt for a bit and go without. This works for a while until they go back to their old ways of spending and they find themselves back in debt again. Why? Because they didn't change their approach to spending money. "Being good" for a few weeks isn't what weight, or money, management is all about. It's about setting a course for where you'd like to be and putting your mind to achieving these goals. With the same level of support you get from friends and family for your weight management, in addition to the suggestions found in this book, you are destined to succeed in your new financial mindset! So, now that we understand that Smart Moms have their financial anchor firmly rooted in frugality, let's get started!

Take a household inventory

This is absolutely the most crucial first step in getting your arms around your ability to stay home. You must know what you *have* — once you better understand what's in your house, you are far less likely to buy more.

One of my favorite stories about the importance of this first step happened recently. I had gone to Arizona to help my best friend after she delivered her third child. As if adding a newborn to the house wasn't enough chaos, she and her husband had decided to put their house on the market and were doing what they could to spruce the place up for showings. For nearly 9 hours each day, I combed through every single inch of the house, organizing everything from freezers to kids' closets. What I unearthed astonished my friend: By digging through drawers, under bathrooms sinks and different junk piles, I had uncovered an entire department store's worth of "stuff." There were 7 tubes of diaper ointment, 8 bottles of aspirin, hundreds of Band-Aids, over 30 cans of soup, countless bags of chocolate chips and dozens of other items, many never even opened, she never even knew she had! We even joked that I could go shopping in her house and she'd never miss anything.

Going through the boys' closets alone, I came across literally hundreds of toys, books and game pieces. Each item went into piles to determine what would be done with them. My friend was blown away at realizing how much money she had spent on duplicate items. She also saw that much of what she bought was forgotten, rarely used, or had been outgrown. As for the kitchen, much of the food had to be thrown out because it had become stale, moldy or freezer-burned. Since she didn't know what she had in the fridge and freezer, she bought more, overlooking what was right in front of her. Clutter wasn't allowing her to see that she already had exactly what she and her family needed.

Needless to say, this experience was heart-breaking, yet eye-opening. Once my friend realized she could reduce her monthly spending simply by knowing what she had at home, she saw that going to one income might be more manageable than she and her husband thought. Knowing that her ultimate goal was to move from full-time to part-time work and, ultimately, to stay at home full-time, my best friend's new goal became getting her arms around the contents of her house. She saw that she had more than she needed and could tailor her spending around filling in the blanks, rather than stockpiling even more.

This lesson is a great one: The first step to managing family life on one income is to benchmark where you are. Know what you have in your closets, kitchen cabinets and basement storage boxes. Keep a tally on a list taped to the inside of the door and refer to it prior to heading to the store. In most cases, you really don't need two incomes to support your lifestyle. Once you realize that you most likely already have what you need, you don't need to buy more of it. Fewer needs means buying less, which means needing less money, which is the concept behind doing more with less. I promise that once you do this, you'll see how easy it is to thrive on one income.

A word here about downsizing. Having just finished your household inventory, you might have also re-examined your living space and maybe even re-assessed your housing needs. Whether you have decided to leave your job, are just considering it, or are on the undesirable end of the employment scale, you'll have to closely examine your monthly rent or mortgage. Since your rent or mortgage probably takes the largest chunk out of your family's income, if you truly can't swing all your monthly expenses on one income alone, consider downsizing to a smaller place, or perhaps moving to a city with a lower cost of living. It is next to impossible to live in Manhattan, for example, for less than $3,000 in monthly rent. Moving outside the city, or other location that allows you to have the same space for less money, or to just spend less on rent or mortgage, makes the most sense. Staying at home is a lifestyle choice and looking at where you live is a good step at keeping expenses under control. I'm not saying that you have to move. Hopefully you can stay right where you are. But if you feel that your family would be too stressed making ends meet, consider it. Remember that the less you spend on fixed expenses, the more money will be freed up for other expenses.

Invest in a thorough top-to-bottom house cleaning and organizing

OK, so you've just taken an inventory, now what? You don't want to simply shove everything back where you found it, right? This is the perfect time to head to Target, Container Store or wherever you can find a quality and affordable organizing system. Remember that when you know what you have, you are less likely to buy more. The next step is to know where to find it. So, invest some money in shelves, bins, cubbies, drawer liners, label makers and anything else you feel will help you get and, more importantly, stay organized for the long haul.

Most of us need help with this, so check out some of the great books on organization. Julie Morgenstern is an organization expert and author of *Organizing from the Inside Out.* You might have seen Julie on "Oprah," or read her column in *O, The Oprah Magazine* talking about the process and benefits of getting, and staying, organized. If you need some help, treat yourself to a professional cleaning crew and/or an organizer. Another great resource is *The Queen of Clean Conquers Clutter* by Linda Cobb. Whatever you choose to do, it's important to have a system that allows you to manage the in-take and out-go every day. It's important to remember why being organized is crucial to thriving on one income:

* Making the jump from working full-time outside the home to working full-time inside the home is a huge change. The last thing you want is a daily environment that doesn't work well. When your office, or cubicle got cluttered, what did you do? You took some time to organize and sort through your stuff. You threw away what you didn't need anymore, found a place for those items you had to save, and hopefully designed a system to better manage all the incoming mail and projects, right? (Yeah, right.) Well, the same holds true for the stay-at-home mom's office, which is the original "home-office"! Just because you changed office locations doesn't mean that you can't set up a working and storage space that will maximize your time and effort. Your new office should have the same structure and flow as your old office. A place for everything and everything in its place, right?

* Since you'll be in your house and car more often, you'll need to have a way to access your essentials quickly and easily throughout the day. This means you have to be organized enough to save the time, money and opportunities that will be lost if you are not. Create a good working space for writing, bill paying and other mail. One of the things that always gets me flustered is when I spend precious time looking for something I didn't put back in its proper place. Had I just taken the time to put an item away where it belonged, I would have found it in seconds rather than spending half the morning trying to hunt it down.

Did you know that Americans spend 150 hours every year looking for things they've misplaced? According to Barbara Hemphill, past president of the National Association of Professional Organizers, having a well thought-out work space, with all of your tools accessible, is the best defense against wasting time. It can also be said that being organized is the single biggest thing you can do to actually gain more time out of every day. The same goes for having a way to manage the flow of all the mail, packages, groceries and projects that come into the house each day. Americans receive more than 2,700 pieces of unsolicited mail each year. About this onslaught of mail, Barbara adds that "...people never use 80% of what they decide to keep." She recommends that you include in your work space "an In, Out and File basket and a big wastebasket." Such sound advice! When you have a way to manage time and space demands well, your head is clearer, stress level lower (OK, it's really just a dream!), and you spend less time and money trying to make it all work. Between the inventory and organization, you have a great starting point for thriving, and not depriving, in your new job!

 Prioritize your spending

There seems to be no limit on what we want. Truth is, we have limited resources to put toward our unlimited desires. Rather than making yourself crazy, write down your top priorities. This list will help you to make your daily spending decisions. Beth Sawi's book *Coming Up for Air* is a tremendous look at how we can prioritize our lives so that we feel less frazzled, guilty and exhausted every day. So often, women say "I have no time" and feel pulled in a dozen different directions throughout the day. In meeting the needs of others, or by putting energy into projects that your heart isn't in, you wind up feeling depleted and resentful. Beth points out that once you determine what's important to you, all other decisions and requests for your time will revolve around getting your particular needs met.

Let's say your number one goal each day is to work out. Getting to the gym becomes your focus and you decline anything that will prevent you from getting there. With each goal firmly in your head, it becomes easier to say 'no' to requests and demands for your time and energy that take you away from your goal. There is such wisdom in these words! Once I realized that I needed to focus my time on accomplishing tasks that were important to <u>me</u>, I was better able to prioritize my time to make sure my needs were met. Then I found that when I'm happy, my family benefits. When I feel like "The Giving Tree" that wound up a stump, with nothing left to give, I'm cranky, less patient and not able to give my family and friends that "me" they deserve and the person I want to be.

This same strategy applies to spending as well. You have to understand what is important to you and focus on that. If your goal is a family vacation, make a budget and let everyone in the family know the cost of the trip. Stash away a certain amount of money each week, or month, to get to your goal. Knowing that you have this vacation coming up, you'll make spending decisions based on funding the trip, not other stuff. Each time you come across an opportunity for spending, ask yourself, "Do I want that vacation, or 2 weeks worth of take-out?" The late U.S. Senator Everett McKinley Dirksen (R-IL) once said, speaking about the federal budget, "A billion here, a billion there, soon you're talking about real money." His point is well taken. Seen as just a pair of shoes here and a dinner out there, you can find yourself losing track of your spending and not reaching your financial goals.

You might recall an episode of "Sex and the City" where Carrie is trying to find a way to buy her apartment after she and Aidan break up. While she is shopping with Miranda, she admits to having more than 200 pairs of designer shoes, each going for about $200. Carrie is horrified to realize that she has $40,000 worth of shoes in her closet, yet no money for a down payment on her condo. She is literally walking around town on her down payment! Don't let this happen to you. Like so many other people who say they have no time, or have no money. The truth is they DO have time and they DO have money, just not prioritized well.

Set your spending goals based on your family's needs. Obviously, you have your fixed expenses such as rent or mortgage, car payment, etc. What you should focus on are your variable expenses, the daily or monthly purchases you usually don't give much thought to. Try keeping a spending journal. If you were starting a weight management program, one of the first things you might do is write down everything you eat. The same approach applies to spending. My husband, Dave, has been such a source of inspiration for me on this. Dave has kept a record of every dollar he has spent, and on what purchases, since 1991. Hard to believe (& maybe just a little on the verge of obsessive), but true. Dave will begin each day by counting what is in his wallet. At the end of the day, he will count what he has left and write down what he bought. Whether it was a $3 shoe shine, or a plane ticket, Dave knows exactly where his money goes. At the end of each month, Dave then tallies up what he spent in each category (food, baby, gifting, etc.). This method also allows us to see our spending over the course of several years, seeing where we have increased, or decreased. We have a goal of keeping certain areas of spending to a certain dollar amount each month and this is a tremendous help to us in prioritizing our spending. If we know we'll have a big purchase or repair coming up, we tighten other categories of spending so we don't exceed our monthly budget. Having spending priorities will give you the financial compass you need to thrive on one income. I guarantee it!

 ## Choose an affordable indulgence

Ah, saved the best for last! All save and no spend makes Jane a dull girl. All that planning and comparison shopping can take its toll on even the savviest of spenders. Every person needs to have that ONE thing — imported chocolate, spa treatments, time alone — that brings pleasure, sanity and fulfillment. Constantly depriving yourself of these simple pleasures, or necessities, is the surest way not only to be miserable, but also to resent your new lifestyle. Everyone needs to have something special just for themselves. Even Warren Buffet allows himself an indulgence: luxury air travel. The frugal Buffet owns a Gulfstream IV-SP jet named "The Indefensible."

When you had two incomes, affording these indulgences might not have been a consideration. Now that you're relying on one income, however, you have to rethink (*not* do without) every expense. As you are prioritizing spending, make sure that you leave room for your affordable indulgence. When mom's happy, everyone's happy! Make sure you have absolutely NO guilt about spending money on these items and see them as your way of keeping balance.

CHAPTER 2

Food, Glorious Food!

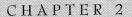

"Live, love, eat!"

—WOLFGANG PUCK

Food. We love it. We need it. A girl's gotta eat, right? Budgeting for food can be a challenge though, as it can seem as there are so many unknowns: What are your social plans? Will you entertain? What are your seasonal preferences? Are the kids going to be home more than usual? These variables can make for a shaky trip to the store, or visit to a restaurant, but if you have a well thought-out plan, you'll be able to get what you need, enjoy yourself and save time as well as money.

In this chapter of the book, I've broken down food into two different categories: grocery shopping and dining out. Let's take a spin through the grocery store first and then head out to eat.

Grocery shopping. Sounds simple enough, right? Walk in, buy what you need (or want), pay and go. How many times have you gone into the store for "just a few things" and walked out with 4 bags and $100 worth of purchases? Did you know the average American family of 4 spends about $5,700 per year on groceries? That's quite a bit of money if you don't spend it wisely. You get the groceries home and put away and you're still not sure of what you've bought. (Worse yet, we often end up throwing away much of what we bought!) We've all done that. Why? It's usually a lack of planning, or running short on time or a hundred other reasons. The point is that it doesn't have to be this way.

Here are a few guidelines that have helped me maximize our grocery budget and can help you, too.

Have a shopping plan

Pick one day of the week, or two if that works better for your family, that you will go grocery shopping. Running into the store for those few things several times per week will put a real damper in your budget (just like hitting the ATM for that daily dose of cash). Grocery stores know this and it's one of the reasons that almost every dairy department in the country is located in the rear of the store. As a result, you physically have to walk through the aisles to find that gallon of milk you are dashing in to get. While on your way back from the dairy case, you come across some cookies here, a can of this there and before you know it, your arms are full of purchases you hadn't intended to make.

Also, make a list. Sounds easy enough, but you have to actually bring the list with you to the store. Not only will you remember what you need, you'll be able to shop faster. (This is key with a fussy toddler!)

Joe Schwarz, general manager of the Dominick's store in Evanston, Illinois, has some great recommendations to help you plan your shopping trip. First, Joe says, start by planning your dinners with the "center of the plate" items and build from there. Center of the plate refers to the meat, chicken or other focal point of the meal. Add veggies and starches to complete the plate. This helps to create your shopping list, as well as saving time in each department. Rather than lingering over the various sections within the store, all of your plate options will be within your reach. While you're getting your pasta, just a few feet down you'll find the rice you need for the next day's dinner and the box of au gratin potatoes. Same goes for the produce and meat sections.

Next, Joe says that you can approach your weekly food budget like a pie — break up your amount into percentages. For example, if you have $100 to spend, allocate $10 for meat, $15 for produce, etc., as your family prefers. This way, you can easily keep track of what you spend and be aware of your department limit. As your needs change, you can change the breakdown and make it work however you'd like. Finally, Joe recommends that you not be rushed. Not only will this lower your stress level, you'll be able to see all the specials and compare prices.

With 26 years in the business, Joe sure knows his stuff. He's seen it all and knows the tricks of the trade. You'll see more of Joe's wisdom throughout this chapter.

Don't shop when you're hungry

We've heard this before and know it's true. Not only are we not thinking rationally on an empty stomach, we're less patient (& pleasant). This is a surefire way to sabotage the best of intentions, not to mention diets. Those mini-muffins look really good to a hungry pair of eyes at 5:30 at night — hey, easy to pop in your mouth in the car, right? Tide me over until dinner, you say to yourself. There is nothing wrong with this *on occasion*. This is not something that you should make a habit of (remember spending is like eating). Despite the best-laid plans, each of us has those days when we just can't get it together. No worries! Just know that it is the exception and not the rule. This is also another example of how eating and spending are so similar.

Our friend Joe Schwarz confirms that the busiest hours for the grocery store are between 4-7 P.M. each day. It's probably also when you are the most crunched for time — on the way to pick up the kids, dry cleaning, dropping off whatever. Keep some snacks in your purse or car and munch on the way to the store. It sure beats filling your cart with all those boxes of junk food that look mighty appealing when you're ravenous! Once, I dashed into the grocery store around 7:30 P.M. coming back from a meeting. I hadn't eaten since lunch and was so hungry I would have eaten Styrofoam had it been offered to me. By the time I checked out, I had already dug into a box of brown sugar Pop Tarts I had been craving, a bag of Sour Cream and Onion Ruffles and had downed a pint of chocolate milk, all before I hit the car. So much for not overspending, not to mention overeating!

Comparison Shop

We all have our favorite grocery stores and there is something to be said for loyalty and convenience. It is important, though, to know what your other options are. For years, I was a die-hard customer of one of the 2 prominent grocery chains in the Chicago area. I didn't even think of setting foot in another store. I was too comfortable with my routine, I knew the staff and I felt confident knowing where everything was. It wasn't until a good friend and I began talking about our shopping preferences that I thought of checking out this other chain for myself. My friend was a die-hard supporter of the other chain and we often ribbed each other about our friendly grocery rivalry.

I must admit that once I tried the other chain, I was hooked. Not only was their product selection greater than my store, but as I tracked their advertising, I noticed that they would feature more of the items I purchase on sale more frequently. Like most other chains, they offered a frequent shopper card, extending discounts and specials to cardholders. I signed up for one on my first visit and could not believe the money I saved on the same items that I had previously purchased at my former favorite store. Since that day, I have chosen this chain as my store of preference. That said, I still scan the weekly circulars for specials and will head to the store which has the better prices for what I need.

This is also an area in which you'd be wise to check out food outlet stores. Companies such as Pepperidge Farm, Entenmann's and Hostess all have outlet stores that make their products available at incredibly deep discounts. That bag of Goldfish crackers will run you about $2 a bag in the grocery store — at the Pepperidge Farm outlet, you could most likely get 2 bags for $1! Outlet stores also have Frequent Shopper cards, punching the card for every dollar spent. Once your card is full, you'll often receive a free item, or items, or a dollar amount off a purchase. Also, outlets will run daily specials, not only on various products, but will offer free items with a certain level of spending (such as a free cake with each $10 purchase, etc.).

Plan shopping around the weekly specials

Most grocery chains will have these advertisements tucked into the food section of the daily paper once a week, in addition to their web site. Take all of them out and see what's on sale for the upcoming week -— this is a great way to meal plan. Take advantage of lower prices and quantity savings to make your dollar stretch. Be sure to keep track of the dates of special prices. Many grocery stores begin their weekly specials on Thursdays and extend them to the following Wednesday. Try and plan your twice weekly trips to coincide with the weekly specials. I often go shopping on the first day of the specials and then again on Tuesday to take advantage of the great prices on the items I need.

Our friend Joe Schwarz again says that you can maximize your grocery dollar by coordinating your meal planning with in-store specials. These sale items, nearly 3,000-7,000 each week, are kept well-stocked to meet the demand. Joe adds that his store will often hold "13-hour sales," slashing prices on popular items to increase store traffic. Prices such as 99 cents for a gallon of milk or $3.99 for 100 ounces of laundry detergent have the store crowded to capacity. Be sure to take advantage of these specials, too, and stock up.

And did you know that the #1 top-seller in a grocery store is 2% milk? You often see milk on sale in stores periodically, knowing that virtually every person shopping will need milk at some point during the week. These "loss leaders," as they are known, are the perfect way to bring customers into the store. Very few shoppers will come into the store to purchase the milk alone and leave — and grocery stores count on that. You can coordinate one of your shopping trips to fall on one of these special deal days.

Choose the right day, and time, to shop

There are some tricks to navigating the grocery store to come out spending less. Shopping on weekends may not always be the best day of the week to get the best deals (although, it IS the best day to go for tastings. You can coordinate your grocery shopping with the lunch hour and take advantage of all those goodies around the store!). The best day of the week to get the best deals may vary with the hours of operation of your specific store. For example, if your local store is normally open 24 hours a day, but closes Sunday nights at 8, the best time for you to shop will be about 2 hours before the stores closes. Why? The store may heavily mark down perishable items it wants to unload. Produce, deli, meats, fish and countless other items can be had for an incredible discount. I'm a big fan of heading right for the meat department and searching for those red "special" stickers on packages with substantially reduced prices. Most of these meats, including lunchmeats and bacon, in addition to butcher packaged cuts, might be near their expiration date. Don't worry — as long as these items are cooked, or frozen, by their expiration date, they are just fine. Joe Schwarz adds that there are stores that will place these items on markdown throughout the week, especially if they have an overstock situation. Joe reports, too, that Tuesdays are historically the slowest day of the week. So much so that many store managers have Tuesday as their day off because of it. So, if you're looking for a day that might be a little less crowded, Tuesday might be the way to go.

Deals can be found in the produce department, too, another highly perishable section of the store. One thing you can look for is when market employees are putting fruit or vegetables back into a carton, rather than putting them out on display. Ask them why they are taking items off the shelf. They will most likely say that they are passed their prime and shouldn't be out too much longer. When you hear this, ask to speak with the store manager and request a special deal for you to take this produce off their hands. Maybe you can get 10 pounds of bananas for $1? Or 6 heads of lettuce for 25 cents each? The point is that what is not sold is a loss taken by the store. It would rather unload items at a loss than have extra on hand.

So you ask yourself, "What would I do with 6 heads of lettuce or 10 pounds of bananas?" Here is another key to a win-win situation. Think charitably. While you can't possibly consume 5 crates of tomatoes on your own, a food pantry, homeless shelter or other organization which provides meal assistance would love to see your contribution come walking through its door. Fresh produce is rarely seen in these need-based organizations, where shelf-stable foods are the norm. Your sharp deal at the grocery store might just supply an entire night's worth of snacks, or meals, for countless people. And your contribution is tax-deductible. Just save your grocery receipt and include it with your tax returns.

Set aside one day a week to cook the upcoming week's meals

OK, so it's not grocery shopping, but it is grocery-related. Once you have done your shopping, the next step is to make what you'll need for the week ahead. Not only will you save time and effort, you'll reduce the hectic 5-7 P.M. time at home by not worrying about what's for dinner, making it or waiting for the delivery man to show.

Think of Thanksgiving dinner. You cook a turkey and you're eating every kind of turkey leftover under the sun. That's not all bad. Sure, you can only eat so much turkey casserole, but the concept is a good one. Choose foods that you can use a lot. A roast can easily become beef stew the next day, chicken breasts can make great chicken salad sandwiches for lunch later in the week and leftover pasta noodles can do double duty in just about any soup.

Once you have prepared the food, keep it stocked in the freezer. Having a complete meal in an individual container is an even better way to meet the demands of the crazy, unpredictable evening family schedule. If you haven't tried them already, the Glad or Ziploc brands of containers allow you to go from freezer to oven to table all in the same dish — fabulous! They come in mini and pan sizes, so you'll find a container for just about any job you have. No fuss and very little cleanup. Add a salad and bread and you have yourself a low-effort, high-taste meal and all for little money! Cook once, eat twice is a good way to save time, money and your sanity.

 # 11 Think Big

By big, I don't necessarily mean heading to Costco or Sam's Club, although that is a great way to go if you have the storage space. Rather, it means passing up the individually wrapped sizes of items like cookies and crackers in favor of their larger-sized counterparts. There's a reason why you don't do your weekly shopping at 7-11! Single-sized items are definitely more convenient, but remember that convenience costs. These smaller-sized servings can be great for families on the go, or for after-sport snacks. However, you can save substantially by having a large box of crackers that you keep in the car, rather than buying individually-wrapped servings. Or, if you have a little more time, create individual servings of your own by taking snack-sized Ziploc bags and bringing them along for rides, or tossing them into lunches. The same can be said for juices, veggies or even frozen foods.

When shopping, just check the store label for the price *per ounce*. This will let you know if the price for one box of crackers is really better than another sized box. Let's say that you see 2 boxes of saltines next to each other. On one hand, there is the large box containing the four sleeves of crackers we all know about. Next to it is a single-sleeve box of crackers. The price for the larger box will come out to be less cost per ounce than the smaller box. Why? There are literally 4 times as many crackers in the larger box. Going with the larger-sized box is the better way to go to get more for your money. Use this method with cans, bottles and bags of just about every kind of food. Don't be fooled by sale prices — if the cost per ounce is still lower with a brand that is not on special, stick with it.

A word of caution about superstores: If you're not careful, you'll actually wind up wasting more money than you'll save. That 5 pound jar of mayonnaise might look like a great deal, but when you end up throwing half of it out when it goes bad (or it doesn't fit in your fridge!), you just lost half your money. Know what you need, know what you use and buy as needed.

These suggestions for maximizing your grocery dollars allow you to choose from different ways to save. If you don't have the time to dedicate to cost-saving ideas, by all means, go with the time-saving grocery items, and make up the difference elsewhere.

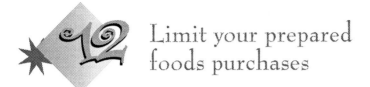 Limit your prepared foods purchases

Throughout the book, we talk about not only saving money, but time as well. There are so many great convenience foods on the market today, our grandmothers would be envious of how good we have it! Whether it is a fully cooked meal ready to be dished out at home, or pre-cut veggies ready for the stove, we have tons of help in getting food on the table. As a rule, the more convenience you want, the more you'll pay. There are some ways to have your cake and eat it, too, though. Remember my motto: "Don't go without, get it for less."

Did you know companies sell the exact same items but in different packaging? Take the deli counter for example. That cheese in the deli at $5.99 per pound can be found in the refrigerated or dairy section pre-sliced in the company's own packaging for about half the price. Hard to believe, but it's true. The same goes for lunchmeat. Make the smarter move and head to the lunchmeat and cheese section and save a bundle! Look for red clearance stickers on these packaged goods, too. As long as meat or cheese is used, or frozen, by the expiration date, it's fine. And again, peace of mind comes from knowing you have a stocked freezer ready to go for dinner!

The most dangerous place to be just might be the specialty deli counter. Oh how I would love to have these amazing feasts every day! But I would no sooner pay $18.99 for a pound of gourmet chicken salad than I would grow a second head. As an occasional treat, or for a party sure, but not as a regular expense. These prepared foods can really sabotage your budget, so just be careful how much you spend when you go.

 Coupons

Did you know that September is National Coupon Month? Apparently, coupons are so significant they deserve being honored with their own month! Over the course of a year, about 75% of American homes save as much as $800-1,000 by clipping coupons. According to the Promotion Marketing Association, in 2000 alone, consumers saved $3.6 billion nationwide. It might also surprise you to know that the highest percentage of coupon use is in homes whose income is between $50,000-76,000 per year and that the age group with the highest percentage usage is 35-44. Additionally, the higher the level of education completed, the greater the coupon usage. New Englanders ranked the highest in coupon redemption, while those living on the West Coast have the least. Lastly, the #1 category in coupon redemption is household cleaners, while the category with the highest area of growth is disposable diapers.

Using coupons as a means of bringing down your costs goes without saying. Even the savviest of bargain shoppers can get better at using coupons, however, and here's how our family goes about getting the most out of them:

First, be sure to check your daily and Sunday newspaper, local circulars and mailers for coupons of any kind. Keep a special eye out for coupons offering free items, such as a new product, or a 2-for-1. When you see a coupon you know you'll use, clip it out right away. Don't put it aside and say you'll get to it later. I keep a pair of scissors and paper clips beside me as I go through the coupon section of the Sunday paper (which, some weeks, I can't get to until Tuesday!).

Keep your coupons in a central place. I use a Ziploc bag, with coupons separated into product categories: household cleaning, baby products, food and toiletries. It is essential to see exactly what you have and to make sure that you go through your pile of coupons regularly and rotate the expired ones out and new ones in. Try and set aside one day a month to do this, maybe the day that you pay bills.

Watch for expiration dates. There are some stores that will, flat out, not honor expired coupons. Ask the manager to clarify the store policy for you.

Ask about doubling. Some stores still offer this great way to save, but only on certain days. Check with the store manager. Depending on the coupon, you might only get the face value, rather than doubling, for coupons that are more than $1 off.

Look for ways to double up on your coupons, too. For example, buy an item when the store has it on sale, and use a manufacturer's coupon AND a store-issued coupon all for the same purchase. Joe Schwarz stresses this is the very best strategy to stretch your grocery dollar. I recently took $28 off a grocery bill of $100 by combining my coupons in just this way.

 Don't buy an item unless it's on sale

Obviously we know what items we'd like to purchase, but if they are not sold at a reduced price, we generally take a pass. Exceptions are on milk, produce and a few other daily necessities that are not marked down as often. When the item is on sale, using coupons allows us to save even more. Knowing that we don't buy an item unless it is at a discounted price means that when we see that item reduced in cost, we anticipate what we'll need for the next month and buy enough to get us through.

This holds especially true for items that are new to market. As a rule, I wait until the new product goes on sale, or until there is an in-store demo, before I buy it. With a product launch, most manufacturers will issue coupons to entice buying. Once the coupon appears, or the store puts it on sale (hopefully both at the same time), then I'll try it.

A word about buying something you DON'T need at the time although it's on sale. There are items that make sense to keep on hand in the house, among them children's medicine. Stock up on infant and children's aspirin and other medication when the price is good. When illness does arise, you'll be able to head straight to the medicine cabinet, rather than running out to find a 24-hour store for that Children's Advil that would bring down your little one's fever at 3 A.M.

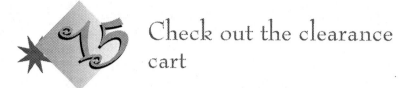

Check out the clearance cart

Admit it — you've strolled by those clearance carts in your grocery store. You might have even peeked in. But have you taken the plunge and bought items you've seen? Most every grocery store has one and it's usually located in the back aisle, by the storeroom. Whether we admit it or not, we've all rummaged through it, maybe even a little embarrassed to be seen doing it. Why? We all want a good deal. And it's not all dented cans and stale cereal anymore.

One of the best times to sort through this clearance cart is after a national, or religious, holiday. You'll find everything from holiday wrapping paper and graduation party supplies to cookies and candy. Again, this is a great opportunity to stock up. And if you don't mind eating red, white and blue striped cookies on July 5th, you'll have yourself a great tasting Independence Day treat for half the price! Our boys routinely eat off of St. Patrick's Day party plates in August. Who cares? The boys love the bright colors and clean-up is a snap for me! I once found, in mid-January, boxes of 10 holiday greeting cards for 5 cents a box — I bought more than a dozen of them! So, for essentially 60 cents, I had purchased enough greeting cards to last me two Christmas seasons. The recipients of these cards were none the wiser and I loved the fact that it cost me more to mail the cards than I paid for the cards themselves!

I buy most of my party supplies from these carts throughout the year. As long as they wear well, I use them for the following year. I make sure I have plenty of storage space in our closet for the stuffed bunnies and baskets with grass I find the days following Easter. While I don't buy the candy a year in advance, I buy all the gifts and decorations I can. Same goes for Halloween and Valentine's Day. I love that I got a steal on the items, but also I have the peace of mind knowing that I have everything I need in my closet when I need it. No running out at the last minute, or paying full price for a one time-use item.

Just a few minutes at this gold mine can result in some pretty sweet deals. Sometimes products are simply overstock and there's nothing at all wrong with them. You might come across an occasional crumpled bag of pasta. So what if a bag is crumpled? The product inside is the same and tastes just as good as the one on the shelf. Be careful, though, to look for expiration dates, or other signs of spoiling prior to purchasing.

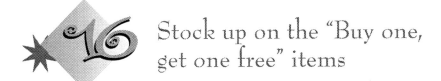

Stock up on the "Buy one, get one free" items

These deals are about the best you can hope for on any given day. This is the time our family really stocks up on favorites. It is also another great reason to invest in a deep freezer, extra refrigerator or additional storage space in your home. Getting literally twice the food for half the price is well worth the effort. The same goes for non-food products, such as toiletries and cleaning supplies. Here again, planning ahead means that you'll have on hand what you need when you need it. This saves you time, as well as money, as you get what you need at a reduced price, rather than being at the mercy of the current selling price when you need something. And when you use your coupons in these situations, your grocery dollar goes even further. Even better is the occasional "buy one, get TWO free." Talk about the perfect time to really stock up! If you don't have a deep freezer, ask a neighbor who does to reserve some space for your stock-up purchases.

These "B.O.G.O." sales as they are called are also the perfect opportunity for charitable donations. Keep the one can of diced peaches for yourself and donate the other to a food pantry or shelter.

Check your register receipt

Technology might make our lives easier, but it is by no means perfect every time. I make it a point of knowing the price of any item in my shopping cart and watch as the items are scanned. If you see an item scan differently from that of the shelf price, note it.

Ask the clerk to double check the price and make sure that you are getting the lower price. After checking out, look at your receipt again. Go right to the customer service counter and bring any errors to the attention of the highest-ranking person available. Here, too, is another reason to know the pricing-error policies of your grocery store. Many stores will refund the entire amount of the item if the price scans incorrectly. Other stores will only refund the amount over-charged, or up to a certain amount. Some stores will refund the cost of just one of the items that has scanned incorrectly if you have bought several (say, 5 boxes of cereal — the cost of only one of the boxes would be refunded). Either way, you are owed money and it's worth the time to check.

One of my local grocery stores had my favorite bakery muffins on sale. Every time I went in the store while the muffins were on sale, they rang up at the higher, non-sale price. Realizing this, I went to the customer service counter before leaving and got my money back for the full purchase price. This went on for nearly 2 weeks and in that time, I got more than a dozen muffins for FREE, simply because the store's scanners were programmed incorrectly. Now, that said, I have been guilty of not checking my receipt prior to leaving the store. Whether I've been in a hurry, or had a fussy toddler with me, I just left the store, knowing that I would check the receipt later. Sure enough, when I do, I find an error. I keep the receipt in my purse and bring it to the customer service counter on my next visit. Once, after I had gotten home, I realized that I was overcharged for 6 sale items. I went back to the store the next day and got a total refund of more than $15! While it might not sound like much, that same $15 can pay for a tank of gas, a lunch out with a friend or a mutual fund deposit. The bottom line is that is YOUR money and you deserve to get it back! For those times when you don't check your receipt in the store, try to return to the store within a week or less: The more time that passes the lesser your chances of refunds. This is because after one week, the item might not still be on sale, and you will lose your point of reference for the refund. Remember that your goal of staying home is achieved in part by getting as much out of every dollar as possible.

Make friends with your grocery store manager

He, or she, can usually authorize things that other employees cannot. This could be as simple as asking to purchase an item on sale in a higher quantity than allowed (greatly reduced items are often limited to purchasing a few per visit) or requesting a product you want that the store doesn't carry. You can also offer feedback to the manager and know that you are talking with the very person who can turn your words into action. As the highest-ranking person at the store, the manager has the power to help in amazing ways.

Perhaps the greatest benefit of working with the store manager for volume discounts and special deals is that you are able to be more charitable to others. To this day, I routinely ask for accommodations on multiple sale items. This simple request has allowed me to provide ice cream at a summer camp for disadvantaged kids, stock shelves at homeless shelters and supply food pantries with much needed whole milk. Making this kind of contribution is the ultimate win-win situation. You can also request a donation for a charitable organization through the store manager. Everything from having bakery goods donated, rather than thrown out, or having refreshments for an event, can be approved by the manager.

Our friend Joe Schwarz once again says that he and his store manager counterparts are more than happy to do what it takes to make and keep their customers happy. Tracking down an item the store doesn't carry, helping with a volume discount or any other issue that affects how a customer feels about their shopping experience is what Joe loves to do. As is the case with Joe, most store managers love getting to know their customers and taking care of them and their families. If nothing else, the next time you're in the store, take a minute to introduce yourself to the manager. Even if you don't need anything at the moment, knowing each other can produce some great results down the road.

Dining Out

Did you know that eating out is America's number one form of entertainment? We seem to define a get-together with friends and loved ones as an event we plan around some type of food: morning coffee, a quick lunch, drinks after work, the romantic dinner out. So, rather than depriving yourself of these things, there are dozens of ways to include these rewarding social experiences without breaking the bank. First, a couple of statistics.

The Wall Street Journal recently wrote that over the course of a 30-year career, brown-bagging lunch can add up to $100,000 in savings. The article calculated that an average brown-bag lunch costs about $3.50, versus a $6 take-out lunch. If you eat lunch out each day, you can easily plow through $30 per week or more, totaling more than $120 per month. Dave has brought his lunch to work virtually every day for 4 years. We estimate that saves us about $1,500 a year. Buying lunch is a great occasional treat and offers a nice break from the routine of the brown bag. Leftovers, a quick sandwich or salad (made the night before to save precious morning time) is an easy choice and allows you to have some control over lunch nutrition and calories. Not only does bringing lunch enable your family to have exactly what they (or you) want when they want it, it's a huge advantage in not needing to head out on inclement weather days, or spending time out of the office in long lunch lines.

As is the case with grocery shopping, *when* you dine is almost as important as *where* you dine. As a rule, lunch is less expensive than dinner at most restaurants, even for the same dishes. Don't forget, too, that when you're out for dinner, you might need to add the cost of babysitting, or valet parking, to your budget. Our family has (or at least tries to have!) a standing lunch date each Saturday or Sunday. We benefit from midday pricing and lunch specials, and often order an entrée to share. Plus, we usually order a meal to go and share it for dinner that night. Not only do we save money, I get to spend time with Dave and the kids, not in the kitchen, come dinnertime.

Eating dinner out as often as 4 times per week can cost you — hang onto your seat — nearly $20,000! Figuring an average dinner tab of $100 for a family of 4 means that you are spending $19,200 per year on dining out. Ouch! And you wonder where your money goes! Take heart: Staying at home doesn't mean the end of your social life, or that you'll never get out of the kitchen. These simple tricks will have you in more restaurants than ever before, for far less than you ever imagined.

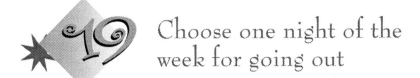

Choose one night of the week for going out

Look for restaurants that have special offers on certain nights of the week. Mondays, for example, are historically slow nights for customer traffic. As a result, many eateries will offer specials to entice people in the door. Giordano's, a well-known pizza chain in Chicago, has 50% off pizza each Monday night. It's dine-in only and after 4 P.M., but still a great way to experience the same pizza you would pay double for the very next night. Another pizza chain, Gino's East, has Family Night each Wednesday. For a set price, you get a pizza and a pitcher of soda. This is dine-in only, too. Other restaurants will offer 2-for-1 entrée specials early in the week to increase business as well. These are just a few ways to experience the same food, at the same restaurant, that others do on Saturday night, without the wait, noise or price! You can call your local Chamber of Commerce, or even use your phone book, for a complete listing of all the eating establishments in your town. Call, visit or ask around about who is offering what and make your plan from there.

Select another night for take-out or delivery. Much like the restaurants that offer dine-in only specials, there are plenty that will offer the same specials but make delivery available or allow for carry-out. Pizza chains (again!) are a great source of these specials, as are Chinese food restaurants.

Stock up on dining coupons

You use them when grocery shopping, why not use them for eating out? And not just the coupons for fast food that come in your mailbox every so often, or those take-out flyers that are left on your car windshield. If you are lucky enough to live in, or near, a college town, you already know the joy of receiving these coupons, especially in the summer months when restaurants are looking to keep their tables full. Special offers or coupons often include a buy one entrée, get the second entrée free, 50% off or eating at a certain hour of the day. Pay attention to the details, as well as the expiration date. The money you save on one meal alone can pay for another meal another time. You CAN eat out at the places you love without paying what other patrons do!

It's not only the casual places that have specials. Many top-notch restaurants offer deals to those on their mailing list. If you aren't on your favorite restaurant's list, be sure to get on it.

Checking for offers on web site is also a great way to find places that offer specials and rebates. This is the way many upscale restaurants are appealing to frugal diners, sparing them the embarrassment of presenting coupons. Great sites include:

Dinnerbroker.com
Forfoodies.com
Idine.com
Restaurant.com

Offering discounted rates for dining out has become a saving grace for even the highest-end dining. Restaurants such as 21 Club in New York City and Olives in Boston have participated in discreet discounted dining programs and have seen an increase in business. One of the nicest aspects of these dining "coupon" programs is that they don't always involve paper. Some are rebate programs, whereby you receive a credit for a portion of your bill. Others offer special rates through on-line reservations. Either way, these are worth looking into for a great night out at a low cost.

 Be an early bird

OK, so you probably don't want to eat dinner at 4 P.M., but these days, you don't have to. Times have changed and so have early-bird specials — they're not just for senior citizens any-more!

The best way to take advantage of these time-sensitive deals is to arrive toward the end of the meal service. If the early-bird special extends from 4-6, arrive at 5:45 P.M. Be sure to call ahead to the restaurant and ask about their early-bird-special policy. While it sounds a bit picky, the restaurant may have a rule that says that to be considered for its early-bird special, you have to *finish* your meal by 6 P.M., versus ordering by 6 P.M. The devil is definitely in the details. But, the more you know, the more you can save. This is also a great way to go out with the kids and not stay out too late. You can go out to eat and still get back with plenty of time left for baths, homework and bedtime.

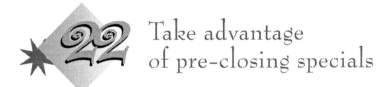

Take advantage of pre-closing specials

Many food shops and take-out places offer specials an hour or so prior to closing. As is the case with grocery stores that don't want food to go to waste, restaurants are no different. These businesses would rather sell an item for half the price, rather than take a total loss on the perishable product that they might not, or can't, sell the next day. Oftentimes you'll find places like Au Bon Pain offering closing specials. Such offerings include 50% off all baked goods between 4 P.M. and closing. The SAME muffin or cookie that costs $1.29 at 3:45 P.M., will cost 65 cents at 4 P.M. Not only is this the perfect time to treat yourself, but it is also the opportunity to *stock up* on these yummies! Buy a dozen of your favorite cookies or muffins and freeze them in individual bags to allow for that grab-and-go schedule of yours! Keep them handy for kids' lunches, late night snacks, or to offer friends who stop by the house.

The same goes for take-out places that don't want to have all those freshly prepared salads and sandwiches end up in the trash. You can stop in, or call, your favorite place and ask what specials they have that day, or other markdowns on food. This is also good timing for you, as these reduced-price meals can serve as an easy dinner for the family on the go, kids heading to practice or lunch the next day.

Finally, look for special items on sale when businesses first OPEN. Most Mrs. Field's, for example, will have a large bag containing several cookies from the previous day that are available for around $5. If bought separately, these cookies can be more than double that price. Bakeries are also known for this, so be sure to check and see what your favorite store offers. This is another way that you can enjoy what you want, have more on hand and pay less than half for it. It's also an opportunity for you to increase your charitable giving. You can ask a donut shop, for example, if they would donate the unsold products at the end of a shift, or day, to a charitable organization. Most stores already do this, as a means of giving back to the community. It never hurts to ask. Many states have amended their laws to allow for outside food donations to meet the tremendous need of feeding people (many of whom are children) who might otherwise go hungry.

 ## Kid's meals—they're not just for kids anymore

Now before you think that all kid's meals are dinosaur shaped chicken nuggets and mini pizza, think again. Many of the meals on today's kid's menus are the same as adult fare, but simply a smaller portion, while others are the same size as a regular entrée. Restaurants have realized that in order to increase their customer base, they have to provide kid's meals to complement that of adults. Additionally, kid's meals are generally all-inclusive, offering a drink and dessert. As a result, you may be able to snag one of these kid's meals for yourself. While this plan doesn't always fly at a sit-down restaurant (many places place age restrictions on ordering these), drive-thrus, take- out and delivery places are surefire bets for getting kid's meals for yourself. If you see a kid's meal offered on the menu, order it. If the server, or food-preparer balks, ask to speak with the manager. When talking with the manager, politely tell him or her that you would like to spend your money in their establishment, but simply want a smaller portion of food than the adult portion allows. No manager responsible for daily sales in their right mind would deny you the right to order a kid's meal. And if they do, they are clearly not interested in securing you as a long-term customer and you are ultimately better off going someplace else. Of course, when you have your kids with you, ordering a kid's meal is not a problem.

One of our favorite stories about taking advantage of kid's meals came on our family vacation to Toronto in 2001. We were staying in a downtown hotel and had wanted to try as many new foods as possible. Schuyler was only 7 months old at the time and dining out at night was all but impossible. Left with room service as our only dinner option, we scanned the children's menu, which had some pretty good meals. Both Dave and I ordered kid's cheeseburgers, which came with fries, drink and an ice cream sundae. Imagine our surprise when in rolled the room service table with enough food to fill the entire coffee table! In this case, the meals were adult-sized, not scaled-down versions of the adult classic. We actually couldn't finish what we ordered, as much as we tried. This blew us away, to say the least. The best part? Each meal was only $6.95. Better yet, that translated into about $4 per person, once we converted Canadian into US currency. Our entire meal cost us less than $9!

On another occasion, I was sharing a hotel room with a friend of mine when we decided to order up room service for dinner. She ordered the hamburger and I ordered the same, but from the children's menu. When the meal arrived, both of our burgers were *exactly* the same size and came with fries. The *only* difference was her burger cost $9.95 and mine cost $4.

Corner Bakery is a favorite of mine. Most recently, I was able to combine coupon savings with a kid's meal for a rare, solo lunch at my local Corner Bakery. On an earlier visit, I saw a toll-free telephone number on the receipt, asking for feedback on my visit. I called in my comments and in return was given a promotional code good for $2 off any future visit (within 30 days). So, the following week, I went in for lunch and ordered a turkey sandwich from the "Kidz Menu," which sells for $3.99. The meal comes with chips, choice of a cookie or piece of fruit, and a drink. I used the $2 promotional coupon and the grand total of my lunch, with tax, was $2.18! I was just as full as I would have been had I ordered the adult-sized meal, not to mention paying about 80% less for it. Now THAT'S my kind of bargain meal!

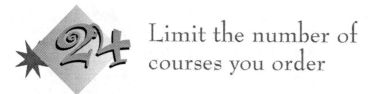

Limit the number of courses you order

While it is tempting to work your way through a menu from the appetizers to the dessert course (especially if you have arrived at the restaurant ravenous!), try not to give in to this. Each course just adds to your total bill, which can easily exceed your budget if you are not careful. Try ordering either an appetizer OR dessert, not both. Each course will cost roughly the same, so why double your bill? If you want to treat yourself to both courses, don't sweat it. Go ahead and do it. (Remember, you need to have at least one affordable indulgence!)

To rein in the cost even further, split the appetizer and dessert, rather than having the entire course to yourself. You'd really be surprised at how much money you can save by sharing. Not only do you save the cost of the actual course, but remember that the tax and tip are based on the total dinner bill. Some restaurants might impose a "sharing" fee, but that's usually just a few dollars and is certainly less than the cost of another portion. If need be, it's better to pay that fee than order an entire entrée on your own.

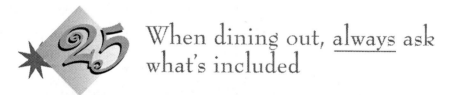

When dining out, always ask what's included

Not knowing the exact cost of what's being served has become the most recent "x-factor" in the restaurant world recently. Many establishments looking to increase their revenue have begun some less-than-candid tactics to increase consumer spending. One of the best examples of this practice relates to bottled water. Many servers will bring bottled water to the table, or in some extreme cases, bottled water will be placed on the table prior to your arrival. Once you have been seated, the server might ask you whether you want "sparkling or still" water and begin pouring, all without mentioning that this water is NOT free. In addition to the initial bottle being opened, the server might keep refilling your glasses from other bottles he or she has opened. Depending on the brand of water, each bottle can run you anywhere between $3-8 per bottle. Over the course of the meal, this can easily add $30 to the tab, depending on the size of your party and the city in which you are dining. Please don't be afraid to tell your server that you don't wish to have the bottled water they are offering and that tap water is perfectly acceptable. See Tip #29.

Along those same lines, be sure to ask your server, or food preparation person, what is included in your order. We all know the famous phrase, "Do you want fries with that . . . ?" Sure, you want fries with that, but they cost EXTRA, right? Something as simple as adding cheese to a sandwich, or a baked potato to a steak, can cost you extra, whether you're at a high-end steakhouse or the local deli.

Suggestive selling is the easiest way for a restaurant to increase the amount of every table's check. Servers make suggestions by name (rather than you telling them) as a way of raising your bill. A server might say, "How about starting out with some of our famous chicken quesadillas today?," for example, to get you to order that appetizer. This is a great business practice, but one that you must be aware of. I can't tell you how many times I have gone into a restaurant with a budget, only to get some sticker shock when the bill comes, which leads me to the next eating out tip.

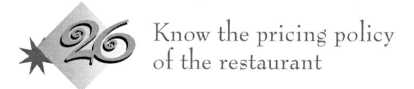

Know the pricing policy of the restaurant

I recently had lunch with a friend at a new place down the street from home. Since it was my treat, I gave our server my debit card (another great way to make sure you are credit card-debt free!) to take care of the check. When the bill came to the table, it seemed a little high for what we had ordered. Looking at the itemized portion of the bill, I noticed that we were charged $2.50 for each of the sodas we ordered! My friend ordered a diet Coke when we were seated and had her glass refilled 3 times, never thinking that each refill was going to cost extra. Indeed, it did. Throughout the meal, the server simply came to the table and asked my friend if she would like "another one." Nowhere on the menu did it say that refills were free, or that each refill would incur a charge. Soft drinks alone totaled $10! That experience was a great lesson in making sure you know exactly what you're paying for. My only other experience with being charged for soda refills had been when the soda came in a bottle (versus the soda fountain; root beer seems to be a big culprit in this area), or it falls out of the norm, like lemonade. So, again, ASK and avoid the surprises.

 ## Order the prix fixe meal

This is one of the best ways to go, especially in an upscale restaurant, as you can enjoy the same great dishes that would cost you more if ordered separately. This can also be the case with a degustation menu. Many high-end restaurants that would normally not think of offering anything like this are now placing a prix fixe meal on their daily menus. Even *The Wall Street Journal* has said that "Prix-fixe meals are an increasingly popular way of discreetly discounting food."

Most restaurants will offer you a choice at each course. This is where you should order a different selection than your dining partner. This way, you can enjoy more of the menu at a fraction of the price others around you are paying! One of the best areas to find restaurants offering prix fixe is in and around theater districts in a downtown urban area. Some restaurants will call this their "Pre-Theater" special, but it is essentially the same thing. Other places to look are ethnic restaurants, which are often looking to entice new diners with low-cost meals, and higher-end restaurants that want to lessen the sticker shock many customers believe they will encounter should they choose to dine there.

 ## Eat only half your meal

This a great way to keep your weight down, as well as making your food dollar stretch. Each time I'm out for a meal, I figure out what dish might offer me the largest portion. This way, I know that I will not only get my money's worth, but I can have a second meal and save some cash at the same time. One recommendation is to ask your server, or whomever is preparing your meal (as might be the case with a sandwich assembly line, etc.) to simply wrap half of your meal before giving it to you. This is a great way to take away the temptation of eating the entire meal (again, another great weight- control tactic), and you will already have your next meal wrapped and ready for you in the fridge. This is truly a "buy one, get one free" meal!

 Drink your water

This is another good example of weight and money management coming together. In most restaurants, water will be placed on your table shortly after you're seated. It's a good bet to stick with that throughout the meal. Remember Tip #25? Not only will you save calories (you don't want to drink your calories, right?), but you'll save a few dollars per person. Besides, you're going for the food, not the beverages.

A while back, I met my mom and sister for a cafeteria-style lunch, my treat. When it was my turn to pay, the cashier said that I owed more than $25. When I looked down at the 3 sandwiches, bag of chips and 3 cups (to fill at the self-serve fountain), I joked that "it never looks like that much on the tray." The cashier, a veteran of this great lunch place, replied, "Honey, it's always the drinks that get you." She was right. At $2.50 per drink, we would have been better off with plain old water. A good lesson from a pro nonetheless.

Also, steer clear from "drink-as-meal" drinks. Whether it is Asian bubble tea or a fruit smoothie, that drink alone can often suffice as a meal in terms of filling you up, as well as containing as many calories as one, so why order it as your beverage?

That said, be sure to have those occasions that you treat yourself to a glass of reasonably priced wine, or look for restaurants that let you BYOB. Check and see if there are deals whereby a corkage fee is waived on certain nights of the week.

CHAPTER 3

How to Dress like a Million for Pennies

"Money is of no value; it cannot spend itself.
All depends on the skill of the spender."

—RALPH WALDO EMERSON

So, how is it that we all have a full closet and still have nothing to wear? The wardrobe of the stay-at-home mom is vastly different from that of the workforce — but that doesn't mean that you can't still look great and enjoy wearing designer labels. The same goes for your kids. The good news is that you don't have to give up looking and feeling terrific. Besides, now you get to skip those high dry-cleaning bills since your suits have taken a back seat to khakis and sweater sets. Bring on the wash and wear! Here are some of the ways our family has the off-the-runway look for next to nothing.

Don't pay full price for kid's clothes, toys and books!

As a rule, the younger the child, the shorter the amount of time they'll be able to wear the clothes. In most cases, a newborn will wear an outfit for just a few weeks. I'm always amazed when I see women buying designer or imported baby outfits. While they look cute on the hanger, I'm hard pressed to think of a bigger waste of money. Not only will the baby wear it only once or twice, you'll be a nervous wreck the minute a drop of food gets on it. Why would you invest any amount of money on clothing that has a short lifespan, not to mention making yourself crazy in the process? In short, you shouldn't. Kids have no idea if they are in a burlap sack, or Baby Armani. As long as they are in comfortable, weather-appropriate and clean clothes, who cares what labels they wear?

Kid's resale shops are the better way to go. My two little guys look every part the designer kid from all my years of buying resale. Chicago's North Shore is blessed to have perhaps one of the best children's resale shops in the country, Hand Me Downs in Evanston. As owner Melinda Kruger puts it, "We sell anything it takes to raise a child," and she's right. From clothes to diaper pails, and Halloween costumes to cribs and strollers, just about anything parents need for their kids can be found here. The day we brought Schuyler home from the hospital, Dave headed to Hand Me Downs to collect a few essentials we didn't have. As always, Melinda was a lifesaver with piles of onesies, a bassinette liner and a few other items we had forgotten. ANYTIME I need anything for the boys, I think of Hand Me Downs first. Only if Melinda doesn't carry it will I venture out to other retail stores or on-line catalogs.

Fortunately, just about every major metropolitan area across the country has this kind of children's resale shop. The National Association of Resale and Thrift Shops is a great source of information. Log onto www.narts.org for more information and to find a store near you. Also, check out the thrift shops for hospitals and other non-profit organizations, such as the local Junior League and Goodwill. You can always call your local Chamber of Commerce to see what stores are in your area and get referrals to other chambers that might have resale shops. Lastly, Once Upon a Child is a national chain of children's resale stores. You can check out www.OnceUponAChild.com for store locations.

After just one trip to any of these stores, you will not allow yourself to pay full price for any of your children's clothes anymore. Seeing a $1.50 price tag on a Baby Gap outfit in perfect condition in the resale shop will swear you off Gap's $36 retail price tags for good. Let other people pay full price. Buy those clothes for pennies on the dollar once they toss them in the give-away bin. This is one of the ways I get exactly what our kids need without breaking the bank. This is win-win-win: My kids look great, I save money and I don't make myself crazy when something gets stained or ripped.

The same finds can be had at yard sales. When scanning the classified ads for yard sales, be sure to look for sales in affluent areas. These sales usually have the best quality kid's clothes, not to mention toys and books. Also, look for ads that state specifically that kid's stuff is for sale. You can also check out the classified ads for furniture, strollers, bookcases or whatever else your child might need. These private party sales are often the best way to go to find new items at less than retail price.

One of the best books you can buy is *Baby Bargains* by Denise and Alan Fields. Updated periodically, this terrific reference book offers advice on baby essentials and furniture. It also provides great resources for parents of multiples, as well as freebies. This is truly a must-have for new parents and parents-to-be! The information is well-researched, as well as practical. Products are rated and offer manufacturer web site. This book also makes the perfect baby shower gift for first-time moms.

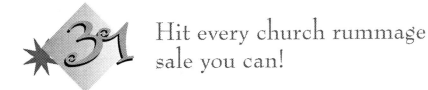

Hit every church rummage sale you can!

Besides resale shops, this is my greatest source of clothing for my boys. The "Rummage Season" usually begins in May and continues through the early fall. Most churches will have a set date each year, so you can plan far in advance. My favorite church rummage sale holds theirs the first Thursday in May, rain or shine, every year. I mark that date on my calendar, make sure I'm available and have my sitter lined up. Some churches may have a sale in the spring and another in the fall. Hit both of them, as the clothes and sporting equipment for sale will be tailored to that specific season (sweaters and ice skates in the fall, bathing suits and tennis racquets in the spring). Check the local paper in a few places for information on the sales. First, some churches will place a small ad, while others will have a few lines in the classified section under "Garage Sales." Still others will list their sale on the Community Calendar, or on a Benefit notice. Be on the lookout for fliers around town, too, as well as signs at the church. Ask around and talk with your neighbors who attend different churches for dates they might know about. You can also call any church directly to find out when its sale is.

One of the keys to having a really successful rummage sale experience is to target churches in affluent areas, as it is the parishioners of those churches who donate most of the items for sale. This is where you'll see Ralph Lauren, Armani, Baby Dior and other designer labels in bulk. What's truly amazing is that the same sweater you bought for $4 someone else bought new for $400! The sweater looks as great on you as it did on them, but for a fraction of the cost and no one is any the wiser.

Some of my favorite outfits, not to mention my best steals, have come from church rummage sales. The first was a gorgeous navy and white St. John suit I got for $6 — yes, $6! The same suit some woman paid $2,500 for, I proudly wear for $6. I had some alterations done for $35, so the suit really cost me $41, but still, the best deal any day. At another sale, I got a beautiful grey Ralph Lauren suit for Dave for a mere $10. The suit retails for more than $600 and fits Dave to a tee!

Many of these same deals and steals can be found at estate sales. Check the paper each week for estate sales in affluent neighborhoods. Many professional estate sale companies offer information on upcoming sales on their web site, making it easy for you to plan where and when you'll go.

As for the boys, church rummage sales are where I do most of my stock-up shopping. When the sale opens, I head right for the clothing rooms, and then go over to books and videos. There are usually rooms with baby and children's furniture, as well as toys. I think ahead to sizes and interests and buy for the year ahead. I usually walk out of the sale with 2 or 3 trash bags full of clothes that last for a year or so. The most I have ever paid for one of those bags of clothes is $85. If the season and size match up, I buy it. The boys have been in Baby Gap, Old Navy and Baby Dior since birth, almost exclusively from these sales.

Obviously, church rummage sales are great places to find just about anything, not just clothes. You will often find that these sales are the best place to furnish apartments, decorate for the holidays, and outfit your lawn and garden. Remember that parishioners donate just about anything they no longer need or want. Don't be surprised if you see cars and boats for sale! This is also where you'll find some pretty high-end pieces of furniture, especially for kids. Forget about paying $800 for a new crib or dresser from The Land of Nod or Pottery Barn Kids — as gorgeous and tempting as everything is! Head to these sales and find them for a fraction of the price. Paying hundreds of dollars for *anything* for kids, except for an education, just doesn't make any sense. They have no appreciation for what the item cost, the item will at some point be rendered useless or will be given away when they outgrow it. I have found this to be true in our house just about every day. Books get torn, videos and DVDs broken, and furniture used as personal jungle gyms. Why make yourself crazy? Buy resale, save your sanity and your kids will not feel deprived of anything!

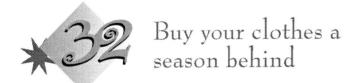

Buy your clothes a season behind

Smart Moms dress well for next to nothing, right? Well, rather than buying an outfit the day it hits the racks in the department store, wait for the end of the season. Remember, frugality isn't about depriving yourself. You can still get that outfit you have your heart set on, just pay half the price. If you buy classic pieces, you'll have them for years. For items that you might not wear every day, like blazers and dresses, they'll last you 5 years or more. As you pass the window of your favorite store and set your sights on that must-have item, remember this: In a matter of months, you can have that SAME outfit for half the price. Or, you can buy TWO outfits for the price of that one! Doing this season after season will save you thousands of dollars, not to mention building a great wardrobe that will last you for years to come.

 Scout the outlets

OK, so you can't wait for the season to pass and all of your shorts from last year are looking a bit sad. You don't have to pay full price for something you need in season. You can head to the outlet of your favorite store and get what you need. Land's End, Banana Republic, Gap and countless others all have outlets. Also, log on to your favorite retailer's website and click on their clearance section. You'll find some great close-outs, especially at the end of season.

Before you go to the outlet, a word of caution: Make sure you know what the regular retail store, or catalog, charges for the item you want, as well as the items they carry. Many stores these days have a line of clothing made exclusively for their outlets, not found in their regular retail stores, are not really a bargain. These items can be of lesser quality, mis-sized or even cost more than sale items in the retail stores. Don't be fooled into thinking that just because something is at an outlet it is less expensive. Ideally, you want to find something in an outlet that was once in the regular retail store, or catalog. Many outlets began as the place to put surplus merchandise that either didn't sell very well, or was out of season. Companies, such as Talbot's, have outlets throughout the country that receive merchandise from their retail stores. The merchandise can be overstock, as well as current fashions. Certain outlets even sell fixtures from renovated stores, including rugs and lamps. In addition to the clothes being marked down by half upon coming into the store, you can usually find racks of clothes that are 50% off the lowest price on the tag. Be sure to get on the outlet stores' mailing list, as this will alert you to special saving days. These are tremendous opportunities to save and the greatest deals will be had then. On special deal days, you can sometimes take as much as another 75% off prices and have yourself a boatload of savings. The same shirt someone paid $28 for a few months ago in the retail store, you can get for about $5. Talbot's

Outlet Stores are a gold mine for bargain classics. That said, it is helpful to be a customer of their regular retail stores and catalogs first. If you don't like the clothes in their retail stores, pass on the outlet. The same goes for any other retail store's outlet.

Think eBay

If you haven't already discovered one of the world's best marketplaces, log on today! We'll talk more about selling on eBay a bit later in the book. For now, let's focus on buying from eBay. Not only can you find the hard-to-find, but countless moms just like you buy clothes for themselves and their families for pennies on the dollar. One of my neighbors swears by eBay and admits that she rarely goes to stores anymore. She has developed relationships with sellers and is a regular customer of many. She buys mainly for her young son, but in the process has found many deals for herself. Aside from the additional shipping cost, eBay is a gold mine for anyone looking for new or used clothing sent right to your door.

The same can be said for any other sellers in the secondary market. Additionally, don't limit yourself to clothing purchases. The Internet community has opened up a world (literally) of options for buying just about any item at below retail cost. I'm a big fan of checking out the used books and videos at amazon.com. To date, I have had only good experiences with sellers and the boys love the stuff as much as if I had paid full price.

Seek out resale shops

Whether you are searching for dress, casual or even maternity clothes, resale shops are the way to go. As you shop for your children's clothes at resale shops, you'll find some terrific deals for you, too.

.The National Association of Resale and Thrift Shops states that it has seen its membership more than double in the past decade. The association estimates that there are more than 15,000 resale stores across the country. These shops can range from funky vintage clothing to couture, with designer samples selling for a fraction of their original cost. *The Wall Street Journal* recently had an article entitled "For Frugal Fashionistas," containing terrific information on upscale resale shops. These shops can carry labels including Chanel, Escada, Valentino and Prada. Many of these shops' owners buy on consignment from socialites and even direct from design houses. Prices are drastically reduced and some never worn items still have tags hanging from them. Inventory at resale shops changes constantly, which is another nice feature. Make friends with the owner and give him or her a "wish list" of what you'd like. Chances are they'll call you as soon as something you have requested comes in.

There is also an incredible market for resale maternity clothes. As any woman who has shopped for maternity clothes can tell you, the prices are outrageous. The only thing that makes these prices more ridiculous is that they are not a long-term investment. It's not as though what you're buying will be classics in your closet for years to come. And with each pregnancy, especially if you're pregnant during different seasons, you'll have to pony up even more money. So, resale is the way to go. In the Chicago area alone, there are dozens of shops that offer both new and used maternity clothes, all of which are fashionable and in great condition. Expecting More in Evanston is one such shop that provides moms-to-be with both professional and casual clothes for a fraction of what you'd pay new in the retail stores. Yes, it *is* possible to be fashionable and pregnant and on a budget to boot.

Don't forget that you can also sell your clothes to resale shops. Whether on straight consignment (you get paid only when your piece sells — you split the sale 50-50 with the shop owner), or selling pieces straight out (the shop owner will write you a check for what you bring in), resale has lots of benefits. I have often found myself gathering bags full of clothes to take back to resale shops. It's almost as though I was just renting them, as I often recoup some of the money I had spent.

CHAPTER 4

Feedback: The Fastest Way to Free Stuff

"Everyone's a critic."

—WILLIAM SHAKESPEARE

One of the lesser-known ways of getting a product or service at virtually no cost is to offer feedback of your experience. Corporations spend millions of dollars annually to find out what consumers think of their products. Many of the products and services we use today were the result of someone telling a company what they wanted, or changes that were suggested to an existing product. Where do you think ideas for new features in cars come from? Additional services offered in hotels? New flavors for ice cream? Consumers provide valuable information that is essential to outperforming the competition. In many cases, this feedback takes just minutes of your time, and the results can be worth, in some cases, hundreds of dollars. What's the best way to go about this? Don't know what to say? Don't know whom to contact? Well, worry no more! Here are the basics:

There are really three very different experiences which allow you to offer feedback to a company: trying a product, visiting a location or participating in market research. The most effective way to offer feedback on each of these is to take the initiative and offer your opinion. Let's take each of these ways one at a time and see how it's done.

 Site visits

This is probably the area in which senior managers are most responsive to your concerns. I can't tell you how many times I have received free products, meals and upgrades, simply by expressing my opinion to someone in an authority position. *Which brings me to the first tip: Always go right to the top.* Don't take a "no" from someone who is not empowered to give you a "yes" in the first place. This means that rather than speaking with the first person you encounter, politely ask to see the manager, or manager on duty. The person you question might inquire if he or she can help you instead. Again, politely refuse and ask again for the manager. *This is key.* The manager not only has a greater concern for service, but has the power to authorize customer accommodations.

So now that you are talking with the right person, what do you say? Well, don't think that the only reason to offer feedback is due to a negative experience. Managers so seldom receive compliments that they are often taken aback when compliments come their way. They are so grateful to have feedback, regardless of its nature.

Here are some examples.

You are out to dinner and find that several elements have fallen short of your expectations. Despite having a reservation, you were made to wait for your table. Once seated, you waited longer than necessary to place your order. When your meal came, it was either incorrect, incomplete or just plain bad. Your waiter was inattentive to your table throughout the evening. Lastly, your table was in a poor location, subjecting you to noise from the kitchen and loud guests. What to do? By all means, don't storm out of the restaurant after paying, vowing never to come back again. Instead, ask for the manager to come to your table, or excuse yourself and talk privately. It's often best to preface your comments by saying something like, "Thank you for taking time to talk with me. I wanted to bring to your attention something that I think you'll want to know, with the hope that it will allow the opportunity to address the issue." Calmly explain the shortcomings of the dinner, being as detailed as possible. Rather than simply saying, "Everything was horrible," give a very accurate account of what happened, or didn't happen, and why it was a disappointment. Give names of staff, timetables and other information that will help the manager understand your frustration. At the end of your comments, always ask what the manager can do to compensate you for the experience. Saying something like, "In light of what has happened here tonight, what can be done?" is a non-offensive way of asking for an accommodation. What is a reasonable accommodation to expect? That depends on your level of disappointment. If the event was a total disaster, with you and your guests being completely offended or inconvenienced, the entire meal should be on the house. In addition, the manager should offer you a complimentary meal on your next visit as a good-faith effort to win back your business. The manager should tell you that your comments are taken seriously and that your return visit will be much better.

You encounter less than stellar service at a hotel, poor conditions at a facility you attend or have an experience that otherwise did not live up to your expectations. Think you have no recourse once you have left? Not a chance. As they say, the pen is mightier than the sword. Write a letter, carefully worded and outlining the issues you experienced. Most importantly, direct your letter to the chairman, or CEO, of the company. Send the letter to the corporate headquarters, with any supporting documentation. You will be amazed at not only the swiftness of the response, but by what is offered to you as a means of making up for your disappointment. I have written countless letters of this kind and can tell you that as a result, I have received free meals (some valued at more than $100), store credits for future purchases and cartons of free products. Each of these offerings has been accompanied by a personal letter from the chairman, or CEO, offering his or her apologies and hoping to regain my trust and business as a consumer. This can also work by offering feedback on positive experiences such as encountering an outstanding employee.

Another way for you to make your opinions work for you is to participate in formalized restaurant ratings programs. Such programs are established to constantly monitor food, service and overall dining experience through the use of 'mystery diners'. Usually administered through a corporate office, most major chains of both casual and upscale restaurants are always looking for people to rate experiences based on established criteria. Some programs may run for weeks at a time, or simply as needed. While you are generally not paid for your time, your meals are free, and usually valet parking, as well, if applicable. Before committing yourself to such a program, understand that your review is taken very seriously and serves as a valuable business tool. This is definitely not something that will fit everyone. It requires completing and submitting your review in a timely manner, as well as being as specific as possible with your comments. If this sounds like something that might work for you, select a restaurant you'd like to critique, approach the general manager or corporate office and express your interest. These mystery dining experiences are great ways to enjoy meals or evenings out with your husband or friends for next to nothing!

 Trying a product

Other opportunities for free stuff have nothing to do with enduring an experience. Companies are constantly in search of honest feedback about their products and services, especially ones that are new to market. Perhaps the easiest and fastest way to go about this is to call the toll-free number on the package of a product. Call the Customer Service line and offer your comments about the product. Make suggestions, offer enhancements or whatever comments you think would be beneficial. This information is the cornerstone of any corporation's success — the end user's satisfaction and likelihood of repeat business. As a result, most, if not all, companies will express their appreciation with coupons for free, or reduced-cost products.

This also goes for any product with which you have had a negative experience. Let's say that you tried a new product on the market and didn't like it. Or, you bought an old favorite and there was something wrong with it. (Recently, I bought a box of granola bars that should have contained 6 bars, but had only 5. I called the manufacturer and within a week received a coupon for a free box of replacement bars.) Call the company and tell them why you didn't like it, or what was wrong, again being as specific as possible. Was it the packaging? Taste or texture? Too expensive? Incomplete?

Whatever your concern is, the company truly welcomes your comments. Corporations routinely pay incredible amounts of money on focus groups and surveys to gauge the success of their products and service. A consumer who takes the initiative to offer this on their own is a truly a gem. Remember, for every consumer who takes the time to call and offer feedback, there are hundreds who do not. So, for those consumers who do offer feedback, the rewards can be plentiful. If enough people express their concern about the same issue, chances are that the company will make some type of change to the product in hopes of attracting and retaining a customer base.

Included in product testing is also feedback on store visits. Many companies these days are offering coupons, or having drawings, to win cash in exchange for feedback on recent visits. Corporate chains like Corner Bakery and Panera Bread provide a toll-free number, or web address, printed directly on the receipts. When you call, or log on, you'll be walked through prompts to rate various aspects of your visit. When you have finished the survey, depending on the company, you'll either be given a code for a cash discount on your next visit, or be entered into a drawing. Panera Bread offers a chance to win a $1,000 Panera Bread gift card, while Corner Bakery has a drawing for $25,000 cash in addition to a cash amount off your next purchase. These are just two examples of companies that offer a financial incentive to provide your feedback. Take the few minutes to complete the survey and you'll save yourself a few bucks, or maybe even become thousands of dollars richer. Hey, someone's gotta win, right?

Referrals

Many companies offer rewards to current clients for referring new clients. Without a doubt, the easiest way for a company to increase business is word-of-mouth. Whether it is point accumulation, or customer loyalty in nature, most companies will offer some kind of rewards program. This can be as simple as asking your licensed professional (doctor, CPA), salon or health club what incentives they offer for customer referrals. Oftentimes you can receive either discounted, or free services or products with every new customer referral. Our dentist offers $25 off an appointment with each new referral. One local salon offers half off any service with every new client. Don't overlook your husband's employer. Most companies offer some type of award for referring new employees, or clients. This can range from hundreds to thousands of dollars. Inquire with the Employee Benefits Department about the specifics and be on the lookout for people who express an interest in working at the company.

Lastly, frequent-customer cards are great ways of making your money go further. This might be the most common way a business thanks its regular customers. Why pass up free products or services as a thank you for going about your usual business? That free cup of coffee, sandwich, cut and blow dry or pair of shoes really does add up over time.

 Participating in market research

Since women are often the primary decision-makers in the home, companies want to know what we think about their products, services and prices versus those of their competition. This information is the cornerstone of corporate strategy for product development, sales and service, and many other initiatives. Needless to say, while this information is priceless to them, companies do pay to find out what's on the minds of the public. There are countless organizations that conduct market research on behalf of corporations, as well as sponsor "Mystery Shoppers." Depending on your schedule, you can do 2 things: 1) attend a focus group or 2) be a "secret shopper." Both of these options are great for stay-at-home moms, as they have not only flexible times but much of the market research is centered on the opinions of women. This is a very easy way of making extra cash and even getting some freebies out of it. Once I signed up to attend a focus group that was discussing diapers. The session paid $75 and was planned to last 90 minutes.

When I arrived, I was told that the group was over-booked and I wasn't needed (much like airlines, focus groups tend to book more people than they need to make sure enough people show up to conduct the research). They paid me and I went home, all of 7 minutes after getting out of my car. That was the easiest $75 I ever made!

So how do you go about it? It's easy. For focus groups, register with a local office of a national research organization. You'll give them information that will determine which demographic groups to put you in and make it easier for you to be selected for a study. The name of the company sponsoring the study won't be revealed, so as not to bias you in any way. You'll answer a series of questions that will decide if you fit the profile of a good candidate for the group. For example, let's say a toy company wants to better understand what would attract a consumer to buy, or not buy, their new line of dinosaurs. The company would have to hear from women who have children, preferably boys, under the age of 10, who buy most of the toys in the house. Other questions would be asked like your age and income level. Once it is determined that you fit the profile, you'll be asked to come to the focus group location at a specific time and to plan to stay for a certain amount of time as well. Once you sign in, you'll be in a room with about 10 other people to discuss specifics about a product or service with the help of a facilitator. Here's the good part (aside from the cash!): There are no right or wrong answers! Your opinion is what matters and you are encouraged to say exactly what's on your mind. When the group is finished, you'll be paid in cash (most likely) and are free to leave. Once you have completed a focus group, there might be restrictions on the length of time you have to wait before you can attend another session. Any considerations will be very well explained to you.

In addition to getting paid in cash, you might receive other forms of compensation. One group in which I participated credited my frequent flyer account with 10,000 miles, as the company sponsoring the focus group was an airline. Other groups might give you free products or gift certificates.

As for mystery shopping, this is an even greater form of consumer feedback for a company. Customer Perspectives LLC, based in Hooksett, New Hampshire, is one of the companies that hires people to offer highly detailed feedback on their experiences.

"Mystery shopping" might include test driving a car, cashing a check and even trying on bridal gowns. The point of having mystery shoppers is that companies need an objective perspective on their business. Employees, managers and even CEOs are never their own customer. Knowing about a consumer's experience buying a car, eating a meal or pumping gas is invaluable to senior managers in any corporation. Why not get paid for the things you do anyway? And there's nothing quite like sounding off when experiences don't quite go as you'd expect.

There are several ways to become a mystery shopper. web site such as customerperspectives.com and mystery-shoppers.com open up an entire world of secret shopping options to you. The Mystery Shopping Providers Association is a tremendous source of information about companies looking to enlist the services of shoppers. You can find them at mysteryshop.org. Generally, you'll complete an application and wait for your assignments. You'll be screened to see if you offer the detailed feedback that is required. In the beginning, your assignments might be smaller in scope, such as going to a fast-food restaurant. As you complete further assignments, though, and your feedback is deemed accurate, complete and timely, you'll most likely be asked to take on higher-level assignments which obviously pay more money.

Who knew there were so many ways to get paid, or get free stuff, just by speaking your mind or referring a friend to a great service provider? Now, YOU do! These are just a few ways of cashing in on your opinion or networking savvy. Many other companies and businesses offer others, so always ASK!

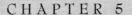

CHAPTER 5

Everyday Ways to Get, and Stay, Ahead

"Necessity never made a bargain"

—BENJAMIN FRANKLIN

Now that you have done the groundwork for success at home, let's talk about some of the ways you can actually save money in meeting your everyday needs. *Remember — don't go without, get it for less.* Through some creativity, planning and flexibility, you will be amazed to learn how you can get your needs met, all without feeling deprived of anything. Here are some of the basic spending tips you can use every day.

 ## Skip the designer photo processing

If your house is anything like ours, we always have a camera loaded with film (yes, we're still in the dark ages of actual rolls of film). We snap photos of the boys playing or friends stopping by and go through about a roll of film each month. Last year, we bought a membership in a national photo development chain near our home. This membership was designed to offer discounts and other special offers throughout the year. We found that between buying the film and getting it developed, along with a photo CD, we were actually paying more than $30 per roll! Even with the 25% discount, that's still more than $300 annually and was way over our budget. So, rather than going without our precious memories, we now have our film developed at a local drugstore. In talking with the manager of the store where we get our film developed, we found out that most of the grocery stores and pharmacies that send out film for overnight development (versus the in-store machine used for one-hour processing) use the same company. So, why pay more for the very same product when you can save some cash by shopping around and getting the best deal?

When shopping for film, I wait until there is a great sale on 3-roll packs and stock up. I combine store specials with coupons and get the cost down to about $3 per roll. In addition, our cost for developing has been cut by almost half. Where we used to pay about $14 per roll, we now pay $7.99 for the same result. Other in-store coupons from the papers can bring down the cost even further, nearing $3.99. We use this same service for our holiday cards and get an even better rate with quantity discounts. Until we dive into the digital age and ditch the film, this continues to be a really great way to go.

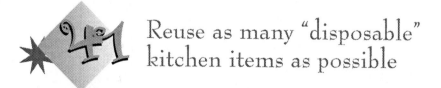

Reuse as many "disposable" kitchen items as possible

We love disposable items, don't we? They make our lives so much easier, saving us countless hours of cleaning. Many of these disposable items can, however, be used more than one time. Here are some of the easiest and best uses of kitchen items ordinarily thrown out:

* Wash out Ziploc bags and wipe off tin foil for another use. The only exception to this is when raw meat or chicken have been in the bags or foil. When that happens, pitch the whole bag or foil to avoid any chance of contamination or disease.

* When bottles of dishwashing or laundry soap are at their ends, don't throw them out, or recycle just yet. By rinsing out every last smidge of soap, you can easily get a few more cleanings out of a bottle.

* Keep the silverware, napkins and condiments provided by take-out or delivery places for picnics and lunches for the kids.

* If paper plates aren't too messy, save them for another use. If you've only had, let's say, cookies or grapes on them, versus a BBQ sandwich, give them another shot. Some brands are so durable you can even wash and reuse. Same goes for straws and serving dishes.

These are just a few examples of how you can get more than one use out of everyday items. Look around your house and you'll find plenty that you can use and reuse again.

 Recycle flowers and plants

When the time comes to throw out that once-gorgeous bouquet of flowers, don't toss the whole thing. Pick through the bunch and find some stems that aren't quite ready to call it a day. You can salvage the whole healthy stem by cutting off an inch or so from the bottom and placing it back in clean water. For smaller flowers, or ones with stems that don't look so great, cut the stems down near the petals, put them in votive candle holders and place them around the house. You'll make that bouquet last twice as long.

After my sister's wedding, I took apart my bridesmaid bouquet and got 6 more arrangements out of it. Using votives, I placed a few flowers in each, along with a little bit of sugar water. I had gorgeous roses throughout the house that lasted another 2 weeks.

The same can be done with potted plants, or other floral arrangements. You can cut off part of a plant stem, soak it in water and when the roots grow back, re-plant it.

Finally, you can always dry the flowers instead of reusing them. This is such a great way to continue to enjoy the arrangement or bouquet, and even get a natural decoration for your home, all without spending additional money.

 Limit the single-use items

As tempting as it might be, take a pass on the "Baby's First Fourth of July" bib, and other items that have only one use, or are designed to be used one time. And while we're on the subject of bibs, Pampers Bibsters line of disposable bibs are great . . . for when you're away from home. Some moms have taken to using these expensive (about $4 for a box of 20) bibs for meals at home. If possible, avoid this. Good, old-fashioned cloth bibs that we've all been using are the best bet for home use. Bibsters are truly a godsend when you're at the park, visiting friends or other times that it's tough hanging onto a cloth bib.

Another area that is rife with single-use items is the holidays. Did you know that Americans spend <u>2 BILLION</u> dollars each year on Halloween decorations?! That's an incredible amount of money to spend on an event that only lasts one day! As we discussed earlier in the book, it's fine to spend money on holiday items. But, if you can, take advantage of after-holiday sales and stock up for the following year. If certain holidays, like Halloween, are your thing, have at it! If your house looks like the North Pole at Christmas, or Cupid's place on Valentine's Day, by all means, keep that tradition going live and well. Just be aware that you can plan and buy ahead of time and avoid paying full price for your favorite goodies.

For everyone else, try and limit the holiday-only platters, sweaters and decorations that can easily eat up your budget. There are all kinds of household items that can pull double duty on holidays, or, buy 1 or 2 things that can be used at holiday time if you'd like. The point is to realize that you don't have to go overboard and buy holiday-specific items that don't get any use during other times of the year. Stick with classics such as silver trays or plain bowls that look as great holding Valentine's Day candy as they do bringing out the Thanksgiving feast.

Travel-size toiletries can also drain your budget. That 2-oz bottle of mouthwash can cost nearly as much as a full-size bottle. The better bet is to buy the full-size bottle and pour into a smaller container. For items such as toothpaste or hairspray, it might be a little tougher. When you can, go for the larger size toiletry you'd normally have at home and limit the trial sizes.

 ## Sell what you no longer use, need or want

There are literally hundreds of dollars lurking in your closets! Think of all those outfits you bought and never wore, many with the tags still dangling from the sleeves. Whether those clothes were for you, your spouse or the kids, you should not keep them. Suze Orman has been talking about this for years. Suze proclaims, rightly so, that if you hang onto the old, you can't make room for the new. Not only will you make room for the new, you can generate some cash in the process. Also, remember that when you are organized, you know exactly what you have. When you know what you have, you won't (or shouldn't) buy more of it.

Once you have gone through all of your closets and drawers (after you've completed your household inventory is a great time) and know what you can get rid of, it's time for action. Round up all those gifts you've received or purchases you've made, that you've never used (& probably won't — who are we kidding?), or household items you have triples of and decide which of the following 5 things you will do with them:

1. Return them to the store and get a refund or store credit. This is often the most lucrative, depending on the store and how long you've had them. Many stores have changed their return policies and no longer offer the full refund without a receipt, giving instead a store credit. Also, if you have had the item longer than, let's say 30-90 days, even with a receipt, they might offer a refund for the current sale price. Without a receipt at all, you might be limited to the discretion of the store manager. If you think you might have a problem, call the store ahead of time and explain your situation to the store manager. Items never used and even better, in their original packaging, have the best chance of netting you some cash. Either way, it's certainly better than getting zero dollars by keeping them in your closets.

2. Head to a resale or consignment shop. These shops are always looking for great things. The most important qualities shop owners will consider are condition of the item and how much inventory they have of the same item. Without fail, I plow through the boys' closets every few months or so for clothes that don't fit anymore. I make a pile of Schuyler's clothes that will soon fit Connor (one of the best perks of having had the same gender born in the same season — both boys were summer babies) and stow them in Connor's closet. The same goes for toys. Everything else usually goes to my favorite kid's resale shop in town. What the shop owner doesn't need, she gives back to me, which I in turn donate, which leads me to the next option.

3. Donate them to a local thrift store. Organizations like Goodwill Industries and The Salvation Army are famous for their thrift stores. Making these donations not only keeps these organizations flush with inventory and in turn much needed income, but is a way for you to be charitable. This is the best option for those items that you tried to return to the store, but were not accepted. Each time you make a donation, you will be given a form on which you itemize what you have given and assign a value to it. Keep these forms in a handy place (in your newly organized work space, perhaps?) and file them with your income taxes. Keep the receipts of items you have purchased and donated, too. This will help you assign an accurate value for tax purposes.

4. Have a yard sale. Yes, this is probably the most labor-intensive way to make a buck, but can also be where you can see cash the quickest. If possible, see if your neighbors or entire block want to hold a massive sale on the same day. These larger block sales tend to have greater attendance &, thus, everyone makes more money (& gets rid of more stuff) than if each house held a sale on separate days. Take out an ad in the local weekly. Many papers will even give you signs to post around the neighborhood for free with a classified ad. Some papers even offer a "Rain Check": If it rains the day your yard sale takes place, they will run your ad the following week for free. And this work doesn't all have to fall on your shoulders (what a nice change!). Have the kids help with shining things up or pricing stickers, or even selling lemonade the day of the sale. Price things at a cost you could see yourself paying if you saw the item at someone else's yard sale. At the end of the day, take the proceeds and park them in a money market

account, or college fund. For any remaining items call a firm such as 1-800-GOT-JUNK. They'll come and haul away whatever you want to get rid of.

5. If all else fails, turn to eBay. With a digital camera and some time, you might be able to get some cash out of your treasures. A neighbor of mine swears by this method and routinely bags a few hundred dollars every few months. If it exists, eBay's got it. There are people throughout the country who make their living selling goods on eBay. These "Super Sellers" are the lifeblood of eBay's success and one of the largest sources of revenue for the company. eBay CEO, Meg Whitman, recently announced that these "Super Sellers" would now be eligible for health benefits through eBay as a way of expressing not only gratitude for their efforts, but also to encourage them to continue their current level of selling. Will you be a "Super Seller"? Who knows? But even if you're not, you can still pass on your old treasures to people who will treasure them, all at a price that makes everyone happy.

 Spend only paper money

As silly as this might sound, this is a practice that has been followed by savvy savers from way back. Except for the change you need for tolls and parking (leave that in the car), put all of your change in a jar at the end of the day. Between you and your husband, you'll amass hundreds of dollars over the course of a year. Again, you can save money virtually without even trying! Believe me it works.

Head to the bank every six months or so and deposit that amount directly into your account. Dave and I alternate putting the money in the boys' savings accounts. Since the money each time is about the same, we think it's a great way to literally spread the wealth. DON'T be tempted to use the Coinstar machine at the grocery store! Why would you give up a portion of your money just to have a machine count it for you? Wait and have the bank do it for free.

Barter

Trade off with friends and neighbors for goods and services. In exchange for your CPA-neighbor doing your taxes, offer a series of piano lessons, or another equally valued service. Offer to make dinner in exchange for an hour of math tutoring time for your kids. Tutors need to eat, too, and a free meal might be just the thing to entice them to lend you a hand.

The key to a successful barter is to think of a service you can provide and match it with a need you have. The world is a marketplace, where needs are met through all different kinds of means. Moms have been bartering for ages, trading carpool days for weekend babysitting and word processing for housecleaning. No job is too small, and no service should ever be undervalued!

Word of mouth is probably the best way to find an interested barterer. Try mom's groups, school organizations, neighborhood associations and even hanging a flier at your local grocery.

If you own a business, approach other businesses in the area about bartering as well. In exchange for placing an ad in the local newspaper, inquire about getting a free subscription. Why not ask about free pizzas for a staff lunch in exchange for printing new menus for the local pizza parlor? Creativity is the key and the rewards are many.

Pay your bills on time

Did you know that in 2003, 35% of all revenues at credit card lenders came from late fees? (And with each late payment, your interest rate climbs, too!) As obvious as this sounds, Americans voluntarily hand over untold sums of cash paying late fees on everything from credit cards to overdue library books. While it takes a little bit of discipline, this is one of the easiest ways to keep more money in your wallet.

Since you have this great newly organized work space, you should be able to have a way of managing your incoming bills. Decide to either write the checks the day the bills arrive, or set aside one day each month to pay, and *actually mail*, the bills. Mark on the calendar a full week to 10 days prior to the bills being due as the date that they should hit the mailbox. Most companies will tell you to allow extra time for internal processing once the bill arrives, so account for that, too. Many credit cards can charge as much as $25 for a bill arriving late. Have that happen a few times a year and you're looking at $100 at least. Wouldn't you rather do something else with that cash?

The same can be said for returning movies and books on time, too. You can easily rack up fees for late returns that can cost more than the rental itself. Even library fines can add up. A library might charge $1 every day a video is late. If you have 8 videos checked out at a time, that fine can be hefty, despite the video itself being free.

Watch out for other fees, too. Banks can charge when the amount of money in your account falls below a certain level. There are even some companies that might charge you an "inactivity fee" if you don't use services or order products over a given period of time. Just be sure to understand the terms of membership upon enrollment. Another hit you can take by paying late is on parking tickets or organization dues. Parking ticket fines usually increase every day past the due date, so make sure you either contest them, or pay the fine by the due date. Some organizations, such as condominium or homeowners' associations, impose fines if monthly assessments are paid late.

Even the best laid plans can often falter. If you find yourself in a pinch and bills are late, call the credit card company, or organization in question, and explain your situation. Ask to talk with the highest ranking person available. If you have a history of paying on time, companies are more likely to work with you. An accommodation may be made by a supervisor to have any fees removed from your bill. Asking for forgiveness in paying late is a great way to hang onto more of your cash.

Use what you have

Whether it is clothes, food or decorating, focus on what you have rather than buying more. Of course, you've already done your top-to-bottom household cleaning and inventory so you know exactly what you have — right? That said, when preparing a recipe, improvise if you can, rather than running out for that one ingredient you might not have. This might not always be possible, but there are substitutes for just about anything. It also is the second part to avoiding single-use items, tip #43.

Check out the book *Use What You Have Decorating,* by Lauri Ward. It contains hundreds of ways to decorate, and redecorate, your home by using what you already own. Rather than running out to buy more stuff, take a look around the house and see what other uses your furniture or accessories can have. That hallway table, draped with a piece of a fabric remnant, might be just the thing to use in the living room after a season change.

There are so many everyday household items that can pull double duty. Just think: A simple newspaper can be used to line a pet cage, cool cookies from the oven, wrap breakables for storage, clean mirrors, shine shoes, protect a table from a messy project AND provide the news of the day, all for pennies. Think this way about each item you have and ask: What else can this be used for? You'll be amazed at how much you can do with what you already have.

Creativity is the key to improvising in the kitchen, as well. Even professional chefs will admit to substituting ingredients in recipes if they find themselves without the exact product they need. Some of the world's most famous dishes were created using only ingredients cooks had on hand, among them Buffalo Wings. Don't panic when you find yourself at dinnertime with your fridge staring back at you with not a whole lot in it. A few minutes searching the freezer or back of the cabinets will probably unearth enough ingredients to pull a family together. Same goes for being in the middle of making a favorite dish. No need to dash out to the grocery mid-recipe. Seeing what else you have to fit the bill will save you money, as well as your time and sanity. Squash can easily replace pumpkin in any pie or ravioli recipe. Orange marmalade can make for a great pork chop glaze in a pinch. Out of bread crumbs? Make your own in about 20 seconds with a few slices of bread, or surplus rolls from the freezer, in a food processor.

 Shop at "Dollar" stores

Did you know that there are actually more "dollar" stores than Wal-Marts and 7-Elevens combined? There are more than 10,000 stores, with Dollar General leading the pack with over 6,600 stores and another 1,300 scheduled to open by the end of 2004. And don't think that these stores are only for the cash strapped: In 2001 alone, 59% of U.S. shoppers visited a dollar store, a 4% increase over the prior year. And according to marketing research firm A.C. Nielsen, 41% of households with annual incomes in excess of $70,000 shopped at dollar stores in 2001.

Dollar stores are now fixtures in the toniest of neighborhoods. Just outside Beverly Hills, California, the 99 Cents Only store reportedly took in $9.9 million in sales in 2002, more than double the average of $4.8 million. Apparently, saving all that money on staples like can openers and dish soap allows for the high-end spending on Rodeo Drive.

Most dollar stores get their products from companies going through liquidation, or from excess inventory. Even the wine industry has unloaded excess stock. The 1997 Staton Hills cabernet red wine was sold at some locations of the 99 Cents Only store. The same bottle of wine retailed for $5 on the Internet.

Budget Living magazine recently asked etiquette expert and author Letitia Baldrige to head to a dollar store searching for gifts of good taste on a budget. Understanding that Letitia Baldrige is perhaps one of the world's most elegant, graceful and socially savvy women in the world, you can imagine that at first, it seemed an unlikely pairing. However, for those who know her, Mrs. Baldrige is nothing if not approachable, witty and up for a fun challenge. With $20 in hand, Mrs. Baldrige headed out to her neighborhood dollar store in Washington, D.C. Her results were quite impressive. Not only did she come up with some dynamite hostess gifts, including flashlights with batteries, she recommends stocking up to be ready for just about any gifting occasion.

Dollar stores are a great choice for household staples. It's also the first place to go for seasonal decorations, toys and party favors. Close-outs are a particularly great time to take advantage of this everything-must-go pricing. The longer inventory remains on the shelves, the less room there is for new stuff. The nature of the business is that a dollar store never knows what it's going to get. So, be sure to stop in every so often and see what's in store for you.

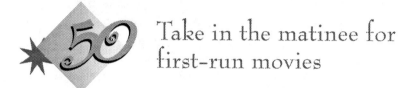

Take in the matinee for first-run movies

With ticket prices hitting $10 in some cities, first-run movies can hit the wallet hard. Why pay full price to see a show that just hours before would have cost you half? Scout out offers from local theaters. Many smaller movie houses have specials such as "Half-price Mondays," or "Two-for-one Tuesdays," not to mention senior and school discounts. Some theaters have begun "Dinner and a Movie" special on Mondays, offering two adult tickets and dinner for two at a local restaurant for a set price, as low as $25 in some areas. There are even theaters that offer child care on site! If you can get your hands on the "Entertainment" coupon book (& actually send IN those discount ticket offers!), that's another way to save.

All that said, Loews Cineplex recently launched "ReelMoms," a partnership with urbanbaby.com. This new program started in New York City in 2002 and is now in 35 cities nationwide. So far, moms LOVE it — many shows have been sold out. This unique program offers a great outing for parents and their kids on Tuesday mornings for a first-run movie matinee. Not only will you find valet parking for strollers in the lobby, but brighter theater lights to better see young ones, who stay with mom throughout the show. Moms pay bargain matinee prices and children 3 and under are free. There are also pre-movie baby activities and a goodie bag. Considering you'll be getting OUT and not worrying about disrupting other movie-goers, this might just be the perfect date!

For second-run movies, you can get by nearly free. Many second run movie houses offer $1.00 ticket prices, with most averaging around $4.00. Some public libraries have movie nights, open to the public for free. Additionally, many military bases or other service organizations (such as the VFW or Moose Lodge) will have movies (sometimes first-run) for soldiers and their family and friends. This can be a great source of entertainment if you are near a base, or are involved in some way with a member of the military.

 Rethink your hair strategy

Did you know that in 2002, Americans spent $50 billion on haircuts, shampoos and other beauty products? I have to admit, I was once among the more extravagant - I used to spend nearly $200 every 6 weeks to have my hair cut and highlighted! UGH! Once I left my job, I knew I had to get a different hair plan. I had 2 choices: 1) get a different hairstyle (NOT the best idea) or 2) find a less expensive way to get a cut and highlight. Enter the beauty school and budget salon.

A friend of mine recently admitted that her hair doesn't look much different now that she spends $75 at a high-end salon than when she went to her local walk-in, no-frills salon, paying just $12.95. Interestingly, *The Wall Street Journal* recently put some national hair salons to the test. The staff went to 5 salons, ranging from the upscale to the lower-end. Their haircuts crossed the spectrum from $208 to $31.20 (excluding tip). The results were surprising. The staffers visited the Hair Cuttery, Tony and Guy, Vidal Sassoon, John Freida and Supercuts. Those staffers who went to the more expensive chains reported that their results didn't necessarily correspond to the price they paid. The staffer with the $208 at John Freida haircut reported that he might have been able to achieve the same simple cut at a less expensive chain.

Another great source of inexpensive talent is beauty schools. Before you laugh and dismiss the image of your hair in the hands of someone who just might have you looking like something out of Edward Scissorhands, read on. The beauty schools of today (now often called "Institutes" or "Academies") are more technologically advanced and cultivate learning differently than in days of old. Some of these schools are downright hip. The Aveda Institute is one such place. It is a terrific source of talent, as well as products. The Aveda Corporation offers instructional courses for aspiring stylists at its own facilities, sometimes attached to its retail stores. All services are performed by students under careful supervision by professional, licensed staff. Treatments are not limited to hair care: manicures, pedicures, facials and massages are also available at most locations. Students are cross-trained in skin care and make-up, as well. It is not uncommon for you to enjoy a complementary hand massage while having your hair done, or to have your make-up touched up following your services! Aveda Institute locations include Chicago, Minneapolis, Youngstown, Ohio, Ann Arbor, Michigan, St. Petersburg, Florida, Atlanta and Charlotte, North Carolina. Canadian locations include Toronto and Vancouver. Prices are extremely low, about $12 for a haircut (depending on length), $20 for color treatment (again, depending on length) and $35 for a massage. You can find out more information at aveda.com or by calling 866-823-1425.

Pivot Point Academy is another chain of schools that provides a terrific alternative to high-priced salons. Similar to the Aveda Institute, Pivot Point offers a wide range of services by students which are carefully supervised by licensed instructors. Prices are also very reasonable, with manicures going for around $8, for example. Pivot Point has also made coupons available for first-time clients for as much as 20% off services. Imagine getting a "day of beauty" for as little as $40! For more information, or to find a location near you, log onto pivot-point.com and select "Resource Center," then click on "School Locator."

Another source of low-cost hair care might just be your own salon. Salons will often give free hair services to people willing to be models for shows, or to give new stylists a chance to work on a new look.

Finally, consider having a friend who is a professional stylist come to your home for hair cuts for you and the kids. Our family has a fabulous stylist who has traveled to her clients' homes, including ours, for more than 20 years. Her prices are the greatest around - $8 for kids' cuts and $12 for adults. She colors, perms, whatever the case may be. And, NO fighting traffic to get to the appointment and NO waiting — it's great!

I don't know about you, but skimping on beauty treatments is just not something that I've ever been able to do. The last thing I want to do is go without a service that will either make me look better, or feel better, often both. Too many stay-at-home moms feel that they have to go without salon visits due to the high cost. I get so sad reading about new moms, or new stay-at-home moms, saying they haven't had a haircut for 6 months, or that they no longer get manicures. Treating yourself well, in addition to looking and feeling your best, should not be optional! Thankfully, there are dozens of ways that you can enjoy the experience, and results, of a salon visit for much less than you ever paid or imagined.

 Rebates

Yes, they can be a pain, but they put YOUR money right back in your pocket. From computer rebates to free gum, it really is worth your while to take the time to complete all the forms and mail them in ON TIME. Don't lose out (remember that procrastination is one of the key things to avoid).

Most rebates will require your proof of purchase, so hang on to those receipts when you get the items home. Copies of receipts are not always accepted, so you might have to call the company and check. You might also have to snip off the bar code, or other information from the actual packaging, so don't throw any boxes away just yet.

Lastly, keep copies of everything you send in. Most rebates should be processed within 4-10 weeks. However, if you haven't received your check by then, give the company a buzz and ask about the status. If they have no record of your rebate even being in the system, you can always whip out your copy and send it in (after you make yet another copy for yourself!).

Work, yes. But, between the $50 rebate on that new computer, free milk and other offers, it really does add up. If the details or time are too much for you, maybe this is one of the areas in which you can barter. Have a super-organized friend or neighbor take on your rebate projects in exchange for something you love to do that you can offer her.

53 Shop sidewalk sales

And I mean SHOP! This is one time of year I actually plan to spend money. I LIVE by sidewalk sales! Around mid-summer, most Chambers of Commerce will plan a sidewalk sale for local businesses. These items are genuine deals and your planning and shopping ahead can last for years.

Take card shops, for example. Hallmark has a commercial where a woman goes to her closet and looks through her bin of cards, searching for not only the right birthday card, but also a new baby boy card for her friends that are visiting. She daydreams that she'll actually be this organized and decides to stock up on boxes of greeting cards. You can do this, too! Bring your address book, PDA or whatever you have, to buy for family and friends' birthdays, anniversaries, graduations, holidays, babies or whatever occasion you anticipate. Buy holiday cards at 80% off. Get baby shower gift wrap for 50 cents a roll. Toss in a few Get Well cards. *If you know you'll need a gift or card at some point in the upcoming year, BUY IT THEN.* Why pay full price in a few months, when you can spend pennies on the dollar at the sidewalk sale? This stock-up shopping also saves time. At the beginning of every year, I sit down with my calendar and write in the birthdates and other special occasions of friends and family. Then I write a reminder about a week prior to the day to actually SEND the card. When the birthday or anniversary comes up, I head to my (well-organized) closet and pull out what I need. No running to the store and post office at the last minute. This saves money, time and sanity. Now, THAT's what I call a bargain!

A note here about Hallmark. Be sure to sign up for their Gold Crown card. Hallmark's Gold Crown program rewards shoppers with coupons and certificates based on the level of spending. Additionally, you'll receive announcements of special sales and other store offers. Every little purchase adds up, so why not take advantage of it? When looking for a card other than at sidewalk sale time, Hallmark's line of 99-cent cards is perfect, especially for kids.

Other greeting card companies, including American Greetings, offer a lower-cost option for cards, so consider these as well.

In addition to the card shops, check out the stores that you frequent <u>first</u>, and the less well-known last. Knowing certain merchandise well before the sidewalk sale will help you not only in selection, but prices, too. If you've had your eye on something for the past few months, perhaps you'll be able to score it for a lower price. This is also a great time to get the kids' school shoes and supplies, as well as home décor.

Most sidewalk sales last for 3 days. Go early for the best selection, but for the real deals, wait until the last day. At that point, the retailers just want to get rid of the inventory. They'll have dropped prices dramatically and perhaps will even accept a lower offer from you. Go the first day to see what you like and buy what you think might be gone later. Then, return on the final day to see what's left. At lower prices, you'll be even more likely to stock up.

Check with your local Chamber of Commerce for exact dates and times. Most sidewalk sales are the same weekend each year, but at times might change. Also, some communities offer semi-annual sidewalk sales. So, keep your eyes peeled for additional information.

Use all those hotel toiletries

We all stockpile those cute little soaps and lotions when we stay in hotels, but do you actually use them? You should! It's a great way to "re-live" your visit, not to mention saving all that money on bath gels, creams and the like. If you actually use only these toiletries and not the regular-sized bottles, you'd be surprised at how little money you have to spend to keep your bathroom well-stocked.

You can also use these as stocking stuffers come holiday time, especially if you have a toiletry from a luxury or foreign hotel. You can also use them for gifts throughout the year, making sweet little care packages. Maybe you can add a brochure from the hotel, or an ad from a magazine about the hotel and include it with the toiletries you saved. Friends will love having these gems, especially if they are specialty brands, such as Bulgari, used in most Four Seasons properties. It will be as though a friend can have the luxury hotel experience without leaving home!

The best thing to do is to put the toiletries in your suitcase each day, so the housekeeper will replenish them. By the end of your visit, you might have quite a stash to bring home.

If you don't want to use these toiletries yourself or to give as a gift, make a point of donating them to local shelters and other accommodations which offer bathing facilities. These one-use hotel sizes are perfect for those staying just for the night and are greatly appreciated.

 Reuse wrapping paper

Sounds too over the edge? Not really. We're not talking just paper, but gift bags and tissue paper, too. If you have gift wrap that's in pretty good shape, why throw it out? This works especially well if you have a large piece of gift wrap and are ready to wrap a smaller gift. This way, you won't have to worry about any tape marks, or anything that would detract from the presentation. Same goes for ribbons. If they're not too wrinkled, why not give them another go around? As long as the gift looks well presented and is well thought out, the recipient will be very happy to get it. Gift bags work even better. There is no reason not to keep a pretty gift bag. Use some new tissue paper (or re-use the paper if it's in good shape), add a ribbon and you're ready to go! This works particularly well with wrapping children's presents.

Another neat idea is to add smaller trinkets you might have found, or bought, throughout the year as part of the gift wrap. Place a rattle you found at a sidewalk sale in the ribbon of a baby shower gift. Take extra hair barrettes you bought on clearance and clip them to the bag handle for a girl's birthday present. There are all kinds of ways to add to a gift's presentation without adding to the cost.

Make sure when you reuse any paper or accessories, or add other accents, that they are in great shape. If the leftover gift-wrap paper you have is torn or really worn out, don't use it. That will just look bad — both embarrassing for you (remember the differences between cheap and frugal!) and for the recipient. The key here is not to be wasteful and to get more than one use out of the same item.

 Consult

Yes, you! Consulting isn't just for the high-powered, global firms anymore. Consulting is simply selling your knowledge and experience. Think about your background, what you're good at and what you enjoy doing. Many organizations, and even corporations, would love to get their hands on your knowledge. This might include teaching a class at a community college (many don't require an advanced degree for teaching), working a few hours a week at home or speaking to a group about specialty issues. You'll charge a lot less than those big-deal firms will, so these organizations will see you as an affordable expense.

Since leaving my full-time job one year ago, I have begun consulting on a project basis. This is incredibly rewarding to me, as I am able to focus on my passions and take on work as my family schedule allows. You can do the same, whether it is within your former industry, or in a completely different direction. The point is to make some cash in exchange for your expertise.

Lastly, don't rule out consulting for your former employer. Many companies hire ex-employees for work, especially if you have a proven track record. When planning your departure with your boss, ask about the possibility of taking on some project work. Explore other departments within the company, too.

After your corporate departure, you can still find work to take on. The Internet is an amazing place to find consulting gigs. Sites such as freeagent.com, or careerbuilder.com's "sologig" link, are just a few examples of how you can look at projects that companies need completed. Take a peek and see what might interest you.

Consulting is a great way to work on what you love, on your terms, and on your schedule, all without sacrificing time with your family. It's a great way to maintain some income, keep your skills sharp and maintain a network of contacts. And if you ever want to return to the workplace, you won't feel as though you've been out of touch with the working world.

Rethink your hair and skin-care purchases

Many hair and skin-care products tout themselves as being the best money can buy. And that may be true in some cases. However, these products often have the same result as their lower-priced alternatives. Paying $150 for one jar of night cream may not be the best use of your cash, nor is a $30 bottle of hair conditioner.

Paula Begoun is a beauty expert and the author of *Don't Go to the Cosmetics Counter Without Me!* In it, Paula talks all about the claims that companies make about their products and offers great comparisons to lower-cost products that get the same result. You might have seen Paula on such shows as "The View" and others talking about the better-priced options for keeping (or getting!) that gorgeous skin or soft-as-silk hair to die for. Remember, the point is not to go without, just get the same products for less. Paula points out that most of the expensive department store creams and cosmetics have the exact same ingredients as their drugstore counterparts. In her book, Paula offers side-by-side comparisons for products that will allow you to see what your options are. It's definitely worth checking out!

There are some real world, everyday purchases in this area that are easy to see. Let's take a look at shampoo. A bottle of Suave, or Alberto V05, for example, will run you about $1.25, depending on the store. With a sale price as low as 69 cents per bottle, a coupon or a "buy one, get one free" offer in the mix, your actual cost plunges to pennies per bottle. A bottle of premium salon shampoo or conditioner can cost more than $25. If both bottles of shampoo have the same number of ounces and have most of the same ingredients, why on earth would you pay 20 times more? Think of it this way: For the same amount of money spent on just 1 bottle of salon shampoo, you could buy 25 bottles of regular shampoo! Depending on your family's size, that is easily a 4 years' supply of shampoo for the same cost as one! Of course, if allergies or other specific concerns prevent you from being able to purchase over-the-counter toiletries, by all means make these products your affordable indulgence.

If you can't be without designer hair or skin care, try Sally Beauty Supply, or another store open to the public, for these brand names. Anyone can shop there (no state beauty license is required) and the prices are much lower than what you'd find at the salon. For cosmetics and creams, try Ulta stores that carry name brands for less. Drugstore.com also has some great deals, so check it out.

 Rent or borrow videos and DVDs

Let's face it: Do you really watch a movie over and over again? Probably not. Unless it's a kid's video (bring on the Baby Einstein!), you don't need to own a new-release movie. Once it's watched, particularly if the movie isn't great, it just goes back and sits on the shelf. Renting a video or DVD 3 times would cost you less money than owning it. Even Blockbuster has advocated renting over buying, asking, "Come on . . . how many times do you really watch it anyway?" The cost of a typical video/DVD is $14-20. At an average of $3.50 per rental, you would have to watch that movie between 4-6 times before you break even. This is the way to go for the indispensable movie that helps tame those tough late afternoons, but for new releases, there are 3 better bets.

1. Swap with your friends. Have an agreement that each of you will rent one new release and then pass it on to each other. Get at least 2 or 3 movies for the price of just one rental! Many video-rental companies issue "rent one, get one free" coupons, so be sure to take advantage of those, too. For classic movies, check out your local library. There is usually not a charge to check out these movies and you can have them for as long as a week, depending on local policies. This is a great way to go on kid's movies that are popular in your house. Also, consider borrowing and lending tapes from neighbors and friends with personal video libraries.

2. Consider netflix.com. This site provides unlimited DVD rentals for as little as $11.95 per month. Netflix offers more than 13,000 titles, from new releases and classics to kid's movies. You simply fill your movie "queue" (a list of movies you want to rent) and Netflix sends them to you. You can have as many as 3 out at one time and there is no due date. Better yet, the movies arrive at your door and you send back the DVDs in the postage-paid envelope in which they arrived. No more rushing to return movies before a late-fee is incurred, no more leaving your house in bad weather or late at night, and no more renting movies that you don't get a chance to watch!

3. Buy used on amazon.com. Remember Jeff Bezos' frugality? Well, it's only natural that amazon.com would extend this mindset to buying used videos and DVDs. You can often find sellers offering never viewed movies, some in original packaging. It's one of the best ways to add to your home collection.

 ## Pass on the premium gasoline

Independent research has shown that the detergents added to gasoline (higher-octane gasoline) have very little effect on your car's performance. The difference in cost, though, is huge, especially if you have an SUV, minivan or take a road trip. Over the course of a year, that amount can be hundreds of dollars, money that you can either put toward other expenses or sock away in a 529 savings plan.

 ## Don't procrastinate

Think about it. When you put something off, you often pay a premium for it. Whether you are late in ordering a gift, or have waited until an offer has expired, you are walking away from savings.

Most times when you wait to act, you lose money. Wait to buy plane tickets and the price shoots up. Wait to make an offer on a house and it's already under contract. Procrastination can be a great way out of doing things, but when it comes to money, it's almost always a losing game.

A good example is the cost of shipping. Take holiday shopping, for example. Let's say you put off shopping (either catalog, on-line, or brick and mortar stores) until the last minute. What happens? You can end up paying nearly as much for shipping as the item you're buying, if they still even have what you wanted. Why do that to yourself? Had you shopped earlier, you could have saved that express-shipping charge. One year, I remember waiting too long to send a friend's birthday gift. Had I just gone to the post office when I had the time, I would have been able to ship regular mail with plenty of time for the gift to arrive. Instead, I found myself with her gift in my hands the day before her birthday. So, I had to choose between sending it regular mail and have it arrive late, or pay for overnight mail. I wound up paying more than $50 for FedEx! I could hardly believe it, especially since I paid less than that for the gift itself. That experience was a good lesson to me and one that I have learned from: What I put off today will cost me more tomorrow.

Look for on-line businesses that offer free shipping for early-bird shoppers. It might not sound like much, but express shipping on every product you buy, times every purchase, can add up to hundreds of dollars a year.

Procrastination can also have you miss out on special deals. Offers can expire after a certain date and you miss out on saving money, or getting some freebies. So, make procrastination a thing of the past. Do what you're always telling your kids to do and don't wait!

Limit the lattes

Notice I said limit, not go without. Stopping in at your favorite coffee shop sounds like a good idea &, on occasion, is the perfect way to treat yourself. Daily visits, however, can drain your funds really fast. At $1.25-3 per cup, not to mention adding a muffin here and there, that adds up to nearly $50 monthly, or $600 per year! Now, rather than going without your favorite morning cup, buy a pound of the coffee you love so much and brew your own at home. You can get nearly twice the amount of coffee by doing this, not to mention having those precious extra minutes in the morning! This also applies to daily cups, or cans, of anything. You can also ask if your favorite store is running a special whereby you can get a free travel cup with a purchase of coffee beans, or other cost-saving offers. So, don't go without the latte, simply buy the coffee, make it at home and tote that free travel cup with you to the park!

Another good way to grab and go from home is with a great new cup from Dixie. It's the "PerfecTouch" cup that also comes with lids! It's the best cup around and even has the coffeehouse look. Not a bad way to have your coffee and drink it, too!

If daily coffees out are your affordable indulgence, by all means go ahead and take a daily dive into the deep end of the espresso bar. If not, make trips on occasion as a treat and break from the norm.

 Skip the vending machines

You'd never pay $24 for a 24-pack of diet Coke, right? Well, that's just what you're doing if you buy soda one can at a time. In a pinch, vending machines are a great way to grab a snack, especially if your toddler turns a bit cranky and you are without your arsenal of treats. Making a habit out of it can cost you lots of cash without thinking about it.

Let's say that the average vending machine item is $1 and you hit the machine every day on your walk. That's $20 per month and $240 per year. When you think of it in those terms, it really makes sense to bring your own snacks and drinks from home rather than relying on vending machines. That is money that can go toward a lunch out, an overnight getaway or just paying down your credit card bill.

Remember, you're not going without snacks. Rather, you're using the food that you have already bought.

Comparison shop

What is worse than finding something you JUST bought at a lower price at another store? Whether it is a plane ticket, or a jar of spaghetti sauce, why pay more than you have to? Do a little leg work and familiarize yourself with the pricing structure at your favorite stores and web site. It will truly pay off!

You can often find better deals on hotels and plane tickets by going directly to company web site. In planning an upcoming trip, we recently found some amazing "web-only" fares on American Airline's website that were more than $100 lower than the best price on a discount travel site. For the same seat on the same plane for the same flight, we saved more than $200 just by purchasing our tickets directly through the airline's website. Other travel sites such as orbitz.com and travelocity.com have some great deals, too. If you see something you like, be sure to check out the sites of companies offering special deals. You can often get an even better price, not to mention eliminating the fee a travel website will charge.

Comparison shopping is really key for your big ticket items, such as cars, furniture and appliances. Saving a few hundred dollars on items such as these is just that much money in your pocket. At the end of the book, you'll find some great comparison shopping web site.

Subscribe to publications

If your nightstand looks anything like mine, you have stacks of newspapers and magazines that stare back at you half-read, most without hope of being fully enjoyed anytime soon. I'm lucky if I can get through an issue of *Newsweek* before the following week's issue comes! Same goes for Sunday papers. As far as cost is concerned, purchasing newspapers and magazines, rather than subscribing to them, can be costly. The average news-stand price of a daily newspaper is 50 cents and Sunday paper $1.50 (*The New York Times* is $5.00). If you subscribe to your local newspaper, you would pay about $120 per year; buying it each day from the newsstand would run you a whopping $832 per year! Wouldn't you rather do something more productive with that $700? Additionally, the coupons found in newspapers, especially on Sundays, can more than pay for the cost of subscribing. Newspapers often print coupons for free coffee, ice cream and other special discounts. Don't pass these up!

Now, the average price of a magazine nationally is $3.50, with many costing more. The cover price for *Newsweek*, for example, is $3.95 each week. Bought at a newsstand, you'd pay $15.80 per month and $205.40 annually. If you were to subscribe to *Newsweek*, you'd pay only 79 cents an issue, or $41.08 per year — that's literally 80% off the cover price! Why pay more for the SAME magazine?! There are so many other things you could do with that $164.32, right? Between magazines and newspapers, you can save nearly $1,000. That can mean affording that much-needed weekend away, home repair or another deposit in the college fund. Besides, subscribing means never having to leave home!

Also, every issue of a magazine that goes unread is money wasted. It's just like that food you bought and never ate and now have to throw out. Take a good look at what you actually enjoy reading and how much time you spend reading. You should consider canceling all publications you no longer have time to read. A great way to read what you love, but not overspend, is to trade with friends. Ask around and see who subscribes to what. Match up interests and work out an arrangement. This works really well if you live in an apartment building or on a busy block. Have an agreement with neighbors that you can trade magazines and newspapers on a regular schedule. Each person reads and then passes them on to the next person and so on. An even better bet is to head to the library and read anything you want for free. Keep change with you to make copies of what you want. You can also request certain publications from the reference librarian.

 Ask for your "wants" as gifts

OK, you have your affordable indulgence and you watch your pennies at every turn. But you have your eye on something you really want, or your kids have their heart set on the latest video or toy. This is what Wish Lists are for!

When friends and family ask what you'd like for your birthday, holiday or other special occasion, TELL THEM! Give them details on where they can find it, price and other information that will help net you what you want. Grandparents especially love this guidance come gift time. This ensures that you'll get exactly what you or the kids want, in specific colors, sizes, model numbers, etc. There is no better way to treat yourself than to spend NOTHING to get exactly what you want!

Epilogue

Well, there you have it. 65 ways that you can keep more of what you have and spend what you have wisely. With a little planning, patience and organization, you'll be able to thrive on one income in no time. With any luck, you have found a few ideas within this book that you can use to help you achieve your personal and financial goals. I hope you'll find these words helpful, as well as practical, and that they provide you some guidance in getting a handle on your family's spending habits.

Spending more time with your children is something that you will never regret. If you have found only 2 or 3 ideas in this book that help you manage staying home, then my efforts to help women who share this goal will have been worthwhile.

As you discover other ideas that have saved you time and money, I hope you'll let me know about them. Making these ideas available to other parents helps everyone, so please send your thoughts my way. Feel free to reach me at critique@sbcglobal.net.

Happy Endings!

Recommended Reading

BOOKS

The Automatic Millionaire:
A Powerful One-Step Plan to
Live and Finish Rich
DAVID BACH

Baby Bargains
DENISE AND ALAN FIELDS

Coming Up for Air
BETH SAWI

The Courage to Be Rich
SUZE ORMAN

Don't Go to the Cosmetics
Counter Without Me!
PAULA BEGOUN

The 9 Steps to Financial
Freedom
SUZE ORMAN

Organizing from the Inside Out
JULIE MORGENSTERN

A Queen for All Seasons:
A Year Of Tips, Tricks, and
Picks for a Cleaner House
and a More Organized Life!
LINDA COBB

The Queen of Clean Conquers
Clutter
LINDA COBB

Rich Dad, Poor Dad
ROBERT T. KIYOSAKI

Time Management from the
Inside Out
JULIE MORGENSTERN

Use What You Have Decorating
LAURI WARD

MAGAZINES

Budget Living

Real Simple

Suggested Web Site Resources

PRICE COMPARISON WEB SITES

Mysimon.com

Nextag.com

Pricegrabber.com

Pricescan.com

LOW PRICE BUYING WEB SITES

Bizrate.com

Dinkytown.com

Drugstore.com

Half.com (an eBay site)

Luxurylink.com

Overstock.com

Shoebuy.com

SmarterLiving.com

Yoox.com

OTHERS

Bankrate.com

Coolsavings.com

Couponmountain.com

Flylady.com

Lowermybills.com

Savingadvice.com

Volition.com

ISBN 141200760-7